The Love of My Life

The Love of My Life
Copyright © 2021 by Ray Burk

All rights reserved. No part of this book may be reproduced or transmitted in any form or by any means without written permission from the publisher and author.

Additional copies may be ordered from the publisher for educational, business, promotional or premium use.
For information, contact ALIVE Book Publishing at:
alivebookpublishing.com, or call (925) 837-7303.

Book and cover design by Alex P. Johnson

ISBN 13
978-1-63132-142-9

Library of Congress Control Number: 2021911185

Library of Congress Cataloging-in-Publication Data
is available upon request.

First Edition

Published in the United States of America by ALIVE Book Publishing and ALIVE Publishing Group, imprints of Advanced Publishing LLC
3200 A Danville Blvd., Suite 204, Alamo, California 94507
alivebookpublishing.com

PRINTED IN THE UNITED STATES OF AMERICA

10 9 8 7 6 5 4 3 2 1

The Love of My Life

Ray Burk

Alive Book Publishing

*Dee is a remarkable person,
I'm honored to be her husband.*

To All My Readers

I have written this book about my wife, and it has taken me three years. It is ideas and experiences which I recall from our 54 years together. It has been a collection of post-its, notes, and pieces of paper, my recollections, ideas from friends, and so many thoughts I wanted to put into writing. I wanted to share with you the kind of person she is and always has been. But sadly now, Alzheimer's Disease has pretty much taken over. I want to share with you about this lovable, hard working, good hearted woman, and how very special she is to so many of us who know her. I am her husband, and have been for almost 54 years now. I am honored to be so close with her. I do not think she would have ever written anything about herself. But I feel she is very much worth writing about, I only hope I am doing a satisfactory job. But because of her disease, and not being able to communicate, I think it is important to explain some of her life's history, and about the amount of love this woman contains. I feel she is a remarkable person, and I think anyone who ever took the time to know her, would feel the same. She is not perfect, but remarkable = yes! With this book, I have tried to show you just some of the millions of things we have done together. I have not explained any of our daily routines, or any of our everyday challenges, because we all have our usual routines. Our world and society has changed so much over all these 54 years, but our Love has never changed. My wife Dee, is still there, and will always be "The Love of My Life'. I hope you enjoy my book.

Dee Burk, the love of my life

Our Beginning

When we, the Seabee personnel, of the Navy's Mobile Construction Battalion 10, returned from Vietnam to Port Hueneme, Oxnard, California, in mid-January 1967, Larry B. and I rented a two-bedroom apartment in Ventura, 8-miles up the coast from our base. Since we were E5's, we could get an allotment from the Navy, to live off base. We had to supply all our living necessities. Shortly after we acquired our apartment, we both went on leave, for four weeks, to visit our families. He is from Colorado; I am from Indiana. We both came back to Ventura, the third week of February in 1967.

Before I joined the Navy, I had purchased a 1959 Chevrolet Impala. Since I was getting discharged in March of 1968, I decided to drive my car back to California from Indiana. My Impala transported me to California, all around California, and eventually all the way home after discharge.

The last week of February 1967, a fellow Seabee, Earl, who was living on base at Port Hueneme, in Oxnard, asked me to drive him to Janet's house. They were old friends from Texas. Janet lived in Ventura then. I said I would. I picked Earl up at the base, and we went to Janet's apartment to visit her and her children. We only stayed a short time. As we were leaving, Janet asked me if I would come back next week to visit her friendly neighbor. Janet seemed like a nice person, so I thought that would be okay.

The following Monday, as I was doing my laundry, I called Janet. There was a payphone in the laundry room of the apartment complex where we lived. I asked Janet, when should I come to meet her neighbor. She told me to come over that evening. I said I could, but I could not stay long because I needed to be at welding school, at the base, at 6 am the next morning. Janet said that would be okay. I arrived at her apartment at 7 pm, met her neighbor Mary, and her kids, and we all sat around, played scrabble, and other word games. It was fun. I got up to leave at 8:30 pm but Janet and Mary spoke up and said, "Oh No, Not yet, you have not met our friend. I thought Janet had been talking about Mary this whole time. No, it was someone else. So I agreed to wait for this person, who was getting off work at 9 pm, then I would leave shortly after she arrived. Mary said she was picking her up, and they would be back at 9:15. That seemed okay, and I agreed to wait. Sure enough, at 9:15 pm, Mary, and this amazing woman walked through the front door of Janet's apartment. She was this beautiful red-haired doll of a woman, the likes of which I had never seen. Simply beautiful. I said to myself, this is the woman I WANT TO MARRY. It was love at first sight. She said she was tired, and I was tired too, but she and I sat and talked and played word games all night, until I left at 5 am the next morning. I went back to my apartment, made a fried egg sandwich, and went to welding school at the base. I was aware of the time that night; we were both tired, but that did not matter. I had found my love! I asked if I could see her again. She said yes, and told me the name of the restaurant where she worked. We agreed to meet again soon. I went to the restaurant the next evening. Her name was Dee.

Stoney

Now, when Earl introduced me to Janet, he introduced me as Stoney. While we were in Vietnam, a Seabee buddy, from Minnesota, nicknamed me Stoney. He said there was a western show on TV in the early sixties, and the main character was named Stoney Burke. Since my last name is Burk, the nickname stuck with me to this very day; I don't mind. And when Earl introduced me to Janet, he introduced me as Stoney Burk. I don't think Earl knew my real name. And Janet didn't know, so she introduced me to Mary and Dee, as Stoney. And after a couple of dates, I explained to Dee that my real name was Raymond. Dee understood but said she liked the name, Stoney, and wanted to continue calling me Stoney. Dee has always introduced me as her husband, Stoney. Some people know that my real name is Raymond or Ray for short, but many only know me as Stoney. I answer to all three: Stoney, Raymond, and Ray.

The first evening Dee did not have to work, Dee and I went to the Ban Dar Club there in Ventura. We each ordered a drink. Dee ordered Scotch, and I ordered a beer on our first date; only one, as neither of us were drinkers. But we both smoked. We enjoyed dancing, talking, and being with each other. That was the first time I kissed her. I have always remembered that kiss! I liked this woman. We talked about where we were from, and the many things we had in common. We just hit it off and liked each other. I was in love! I wanted Dee to be in my life. I purchased a combination engagement/wedding ring, with payments, at a jeweler in Oxnard, $300.00. I asked Dee to marry me after about 3 weeks. I paid off the ring in a couple of weeks, no problem. After I proposed to Dee, and Dee had said yes, I told her I did not want to get married until I was finished with Vietnam. I was scheduled to go back in May 1967, with the Navy's Mobile Construction Battalion #10. I did not want her to hold on to me while I was gone. She could find someone she liked better than me. And too many guys received Dear John letters while out of the country. Plus anything could happen to me while overseas. Dee said she would wait regardless but still, I felt strongly about waiting.

I had finished the Navy's welding school, and military training, and was prepared to do whatever I was assigned to do for the Navy until I was discharged. I knew I did not want a career in the military. But as time went along it seemed to fly, and we were steadily seeing each other. Frankly, I was scared about getting married, but I knew Dee was right for me. It would mean being more responsible, now there would be two of us to care for. But I loved this woman! We both wanted to be together, we would be patient until we could formalize our love forever.

Sometime when we were dating, I invited Dee, and her roommate Mary, and Mary's two daughters, Janet, and her two children to our apartment for dinner one evening.. My roommate and I had an agreement, if one of us did the cooking, the other would clean the dishes and kitchen. We were very honored to help each other. My roommate helped me prepare this meal. I remember, I had fixed some type of beef, along with mashed potatoes, vegetables, dinner rolls, maybe salad, and I had baked a cake too. I also had some kind of drink for the kids, and adults if they wanted, plus I had Colt 45 Malt Liquor for the adults. Everyone had a good time. I think the kids had some kind of game they played. Dee told me several times after we were married how very much they appreciated that meal. She said that they had been eating out of cans, because they did not have enough money to buy food. They all were hungry. Of course, I did not know that at the time, I only invited them all to dinner, because I liked them. And I wanted to show my appreciation for all of them being in my life. But I am happy they were hungry, and appreciated our efforts. I wonder if any of them remember this evening, besides Dee. How I loved this Dee.

Luckily, in the middle of May 1967, President Johnson signed a bill stating that anyone who had been in the country of Vietnam for 12 months or more had to have 2 years of shore duty before they could be sent back again. I had been there for a total of 16 months at that time. The Navy quickly processed orders for me to transfer to Naval Air Station, in Alameda, California, with a check-in on June 1st. This meant that I would not be leaving the country, and we could get married anytime. We had not planned any formal arrangements, but we talked about what we wanted to do. After checking out of the battalion, I drove up California, to Naval Air Station in Alameda, and checked in on June 1st. I had been given three days to make the trip of 375 miles. After checking in, I was assigned to Public Works, plus I had my duties of being a steelworker. Things were not too bad there, except the chief in charge of our department: he was not such a nice person. But I had a great first-class over me, Alex. Alex told me that after we did our Friday morning get-together, I could leave the base if I did not have weekend duty. So I would drive from Alameda to Ventura on Friday's to see Dee and return on Sunday afternoons. Sometimes I rode the Greyhound bus to Ventura. I would go straight to see Dee, she and Mary would let me sleep on their couch. We did many things together, and we made our plans for getting married. We set the date of Labor Day weekend, Sept. 1st, as this was a three-day weekend, and would give us an extra day to get back to Alameda, California, and relax.

We were married on Saturday afternoon, September 1st, in a non-denominational church, by the minister, Reverend Grossitt, in Ventura. The ceremony took place in the church parsonage. Connie, 8 years old, was Dee's bridesmaid, and David, 10 years old, was my best man. Connie was Janet's daughter, and Michael was the other Connie's son. Friends attending were Joe and Susan, Daryl and Linda, Janet and her son Michael, and Mary, Pamela, and Janelle, Michael's mother, Connie, and the minister's wife. It was a very nice wedding service, I remember it well. A memory I will never forget. After the church service, we went back to Dee's apartment for cake and ice cream. I don't remember who baked the cake. It was a wonderful occasion. When all the festivities were over, we loaded all of Dee's things into my car and trailer and we departed to Alameda, California.

Our Move to Northern California

We said our goodbyes and left Ventura around 11:30 pm. I drove all night with my beautiful wife, Dee by my side. We arrived at our apartment in Alameda at 7 am. We unloaded the car and trailer, and then we rested for a while. Dee was a little disappointed in the apartment, it was not very nice. But it was clean and would do for 6 months. The floor was linoleum over cement, very cold in the winter. There was a small gas heater in the front room, and the kitchen was in the back of the apartment. To help warm the apartment, Dee would turn on the kitchen stove oven, and leave the door open. This is how we warmed the place up. Winters in northern California can get pretty damp and cold. We did a lot of shopping at the flea market close by. We enjoyed the flea market, even in cold, wet weather. Plus, we did most of our grocery shopping at the base commissary.

I soon introduced Dee to my Navy comrades there in Alameda; some were nicer than others. Some had drinking problems, but that was typical of some Navy personnel. Paul and Alex were my higher-ranking Navy Petty Officers. Paul wanted Dee and me to move to Lima, Peru, after discharge. Dee and I talked it over, but we decided not to go there. That is where Paul and his wife were living at the time. But Paul was originally from Pennsylvania. He liked Peru, but it was too far from my family for Dee and myself. But we talked about the offer.

Paul and Alex were good guys and looked out for us. I was assigned to Public Works, and I had to stand duty a lot. Duty was usually taxi, and bus driving. I also had duties at our shop, with lots of dumpster repairs. I did build my trailer while I was there, our desk, and footlockers, and some other little things. Our Chief in charge was a jerk, no one liked him... maybe his wife did. He was a steelworker ranked Chief, but he gave the

Navy a bad name. One Sunday, we all had a get-together at the park near the end of the runways. There is a beautiful view of the Bay and San Francisco from there. It was a picnic, plenty of food, and we played games for the kids, and volleyball for the adults. Dee and I played against the Chief and his wife, and we beat the socks off them, and oh he was mad! There were other people there, but the thing I remember most was how angry the Chief had gotten. Also, Henry was there with his wife and 5 kids, whom he called animals, instead of by their names. Henry drank too much, this created problems for many of us. His wife was Puerto Rican, and she would call, and ask me to go and get Henry home. Henry would be drunk at a bar. The call usually came late at night, or early in the morning. Sometimes, Henry had been roughed up. We all tried to control his problem before he got drunk, but he was a bartender. And you cannot control alcoholics.

A couple of weeks after Dee was in Alameda, she went to work as a waitress in Berkeley. Dee always belonged to the Waitress and Bartenders Union. They would assign job vacancies to Union people wanting work. The Union headquarters was here in Oakland. Dee went to work at Wilkinson's restaurant in Berkeley. Dee worked there a few months before I was discharged. Dee only worked day shifts but had to work weekends along with three weekdays. Dee was always a good worker, on time, and made pretty good money. Dee's income helped us tremendously. The Navy was not a big paycheck. Dee would catch the bus on the corner, and it went by the front of the restaurant, so I did not need to take her to work. I did take her some on the weekends. In Alameda, where we lived, there was a great coffee shop called Tim's. It was a good place to eat, and we would eat dinner there after Dee came home from work sometimes. I did not want Dee to cook after working all day. Because, most of the time, Dee would get out of bed at 4 am, to fix her hair, and get ready for work. I always got up, but later.

Dee is a disciplined person. We always ate together. Then I would walk her to the bus, and make sure Dee got on the bus okay. Dee seemed to like northern California quite a lot.

Barry, who was in the Navy too, and his wife Cindy, lived in an apartment building around the corner. Dee and Cindy became good friends, I never did care much for Barry. Barry and I commuted to the base together. A little later, Cindy became pregnant and had a baby boy they named Little Barry. We did stay in touch with Cindy after they divorced but eventually lost track. Cindy had moved back to New York, with her mother. This was sometime after I was discharged. We did make friends with Cindy's mother; sadly, she (Cindy's mother) died shortly after, but she told us Cindy remarried. We also had other neighbors, Allen and Dottie, who lived upstairs. Dottie also worked in restaurants, and Allen was on disability. Allen was not so likable either. He had had a stroke, which paralyzed his right side. Since they lived upstairs, we went out to eat with them sometimes, to The Red Lamp, and sometimes to Tim's.

In November 1967, for Thanksgiving dinner, Dee and I went to Tim's to eat. We both had the day off. When we came home to the apartment, a black long-haired kitten was sitting on the front step. We brought her in, named her Duchess, and proceeded to tackle her flea problem. The apartment floor in Alameda was so cold, she would jump from chair to chair to avoid stepping on the cold, cold floor. Dee and I had a lot of fun at that apartment, many friends, many good times too. Duchess was a wonderful kitty. Looking back over the years with Duchess, I am ashamed of how poorly I treated her, she needed better care than I gave her. She traveled all over with us, never causing us any problems. The cold apartment would be ok until I was discharged. After discharge the three of us moved to Indiana where Duchess would sit in the window, and chatter at the birds. Duchess was a real sweetheart. We loved her immensely.

The 1967 holidays were great, our first season together. I was still in the Navy in Alameda, California. Dee and I drove around, looking at all the Christmas lights and decorations. We also walked around the streets looking at the decorations and lights on the main streets. We had a little Christmas Tree of our own to decorate, Duchess kept tipping it over. I truly loved Dee, and I was determined to do the best I could to help her be happy and provide for her. We did some shopping at the base but did most shopping at the local stores close to us. We enjoyed the flea market, it was close by. I have always enjoyed shopping with Dee. I knew Dee had always been independent, but I truly wanted to share all aspects of our new life together.

Discharge

Time passed, and then it was March 8, 1968. On Friday 8th March, I was discharged from the Navy. I was supposed to get out on the 10th, but that was a Sunday, so they let me out on the 8th. The commanding officer asked me to re-enlist, but I said no, I had had enough military life.

We planned to move back to Indiana to work on my parents' farms. I thought they needed my help. Also, since Dee had no family, I wanted my family to be hers too. They were good, loving parents. More than anything, I wanted Dee to belong to a loving family, something I did not think she had had. So we started driving. I had trouble with the car, caused by the rust in the fuel tank. We were pulling the trailer I had made, and that kept the gas tank fuel splashing around more than usual. I had to stop periodically to clean the fuel filter. But eventually, we made it to Indiana.

We left Alameda on Saturday morning, March 9th. We drove to Hollywood, California. to see Gayle and her daughters. We stayed there 3 days, before continuing on our drive to Indiana. While we were parked there, someone took a box out of our trailer, causing us to lose all my Navy uniforms, but more sadly all of Dee's family pictures, and other things she had wanted to keep. They were gone. Dee never held anything against me for allowing this to happen, but I sure wish I had put that box in the moving truck, along with all the other things the Navy shipped for us. Or, I could have taken it inside Gayle's apartment, but I thought it would be safe. It was heavy. I thought we may need some things out of the box to show Gayle, but we did not need anything. I have always regretted not shipping it with the other things because it had Dee's only family connections in it. I should have looked more for the box in Hollywood before we left, but it was raining that morning. We left Hollywood and drove across the country to Indiana. It took us 3 or 4 days. We stopped and stayed in motels at night. We had saved enough money for the trip, plus I had $500 cash for getting discharged out of the Navy. We saved all we could because we did not know about our future expenses. Dee has always been very good at saving money, very disciplined. Dee is very organized about managing money too. Dee taught me how to do this. We have always pooled our money, it did not matter who earned it.

When we arrived at mom and dad's farm, it was milking time in the evening, around 5 pm. Mom and dad were in the milking parlor, milking the cows. My timing was not good. I knew dad would get upset if strangers came in while the milking was going on. But I was excited, and I had forgotten. We walked in and I hugged mom. Mom had already met Dee. I then walked down to dad and hugged him and I proceeded to introduce Dee to him. She tried to hug him, but he did not respond. He said to get her out of here, she was making the cows nervous. It seemed dad had become angry. So Dee and I went back into the milk house until the milking was finished. I was so disappointed! I tried to explain to Dee, but how could Dee understand. We were not causing any problems, they just did not want us there. It was all my mistake. I thought they wanted me back on the farm to help. I was wrong, it was all my mistake! Dee and I tried to fit in any way we could. Dee tried to be a positive part of this new family. She tried so very very hard. They seemed to be against her, no matter what she did. And I was not on much better terms. We should have stayed in California. Dee had suggested we store our things in California and go back to Indiana on a trial basis. Then, if we needed our things, we could go and get them. I recall that in one of my mother's letters which she sent shortly before I was discharged, my mother had made some kind of remark, that they were doing ok, and may not need us. But I thought moving back to Indiana was the right thing to do. Plus, I had several ideas about increasing all aspects of the farming business. And I thought I could get a job somewhere if I needed to. I wanted Dee to have a loving family. More than anything, I wanted Dee to be in a loving family. Mom and dad just did not want us there.

We both worked hard that summer, using all the $500 savings to get supplies and furniture for the house we were living in. We both were working on the farms, but Dee did not feel like mom and dad wanted her there. Dee was correct and started looking for something to do. She helped clean houses for some relatives. We also mowed lawns for some neighbors. But Dee felt she wanted to get back to waitress work. Dee then acquired a waitress job in Greenville, Ohio, working from 6 pm to 2 am. She did not make much money, took a lot of crap from drunk farmers, and the young and immatures. She took too much abuse. Many times I was late picking her up. I was so tired that I overslept. Dee worked there for 2 or 3 months and then found another waitress job in Winchester, Indiana. It was worse, but the hours were better. The customers were better too. But the owner was much worse. It was an afternoon-evening shift, and I was able to help her clean the restaurant after I got off work. It was hard for anyone to clean because the mops were so heavy, and there were a lot of floors to mop. No help from the owner. Dee only worked there a couple of months. By this time I had gotten a job building truck bodies in Union City, Indiana. I worked in the factory and helped on the farm when I could. Luckily, I was able to work the 2nd shift. I fed the feeding cattle, morning and night on the farm where we lived. Then Dee found a job at the Westinghouse factory in Union City, Indiana. Dee was assigned to do something to electric motors there. Dee is not mechanically inclined, but another nice lady, Jeannettia, who also worked in this department, helped Dee learn the process that needed to be done to each motor. Then each of these motors could be moved on to the next station. I do not think Dee could have kept her employment with Westinghouse, without Jeannettias' sincere help. Jeannettia helped Dee keep the job. And even though we have moved away from Indiana, Jeannettia, who is not related to us, has remained a very close friend to Dee and myself, over all these years. We talk by phone frequently, to discuss how she and her family are doing. and of course I tell her how Dee and I are doing. I also had a cousin, who worked in this department at a different job, but he could not help Dee with these work procedures to assemble these motors. We truly thank Jeannettia for all her help. By now we were both working the 2nd shift hours, only one hour difference at the end of shifts. Because of the cold weather in Indiana, Jeannettia would keep Dee in her car, until I got off work. Dee tried to fit in, and she put her all into it. We both worked hard. Before we left California, in 1968, I had been offered a job repairing trash dumpsters at the Naval Air Station. So we both worked hard towards our goal, while in Indiana, saved our money, and decided to move back to California. There were other factors in making this decision, but relocating had become our goal.

Our Move Back to California

This was a good decision for us, and made us closer to each other. We were determined to make our move successful, and so far we have. Before we left California in 1968, I was told about the job repairing trash dumpsters for the Navy, at the Naval Air Station. And I thought, if we moved back to California, I may be able to have a position there. However, that did not work out. But we thought Dee could find work as a waitress, which she did. But there were other factors in making our decision to move back to California.The atmosphere at the farm was ok, because by this time Dee had things to do around the farm which mom and dad approved. But Dee thought she would be of more help if she went to work as a waitress, which she did. But probably the main reason for our move was two fold. First, Dee was considered a "City Girl". And for some reason, my parents felt City People were lazy, and overpaid. Dee is not a lazy person. Number two. I was not on much better terms, because I had been away from the farm for several years. And the last few years I was at home, I had had several ideas concerning the farming industry. But my parents had their ideas, and they did not want my ideas. But I had learned many of these ideas from high school, in my Agriculture class. I thought they were worth trying, but dad did not. Then Dee and I just decided it would be best if we moved to a different location. Then we both worked hard toward our goal. We saved our money and worked toward making the move. Before we left Indiana, for us to make our move, I rented a U-haul truck. We put all our things in it, Dee, and Duchess the kitty, and myself, and drove back to northern California. We stopped in Ventura, California, first to visit Janet and her family where they lived, and also Gayle and her family. Gayle had driven up to Janet's house in Ventura. Then we drove on to Alameda, California. This was around Memorial Day weekend 1969.

After we arrived at Alameda, we found an apartment and moved all our furnishings in. Dee went back to work at Wilkinson's restaurant in Berkeley. The dumpster repair position was not available, but I did get a job driving a Salvation Army truck. I worked in that position for about 2 months. Then one evening, Mr. Hook, who lived next door to us, told me that Del Monte was hiring. I applied. I was hired by Del Monte Corp., just down the street, from where we lived in Alameda. After we moved to Oakland, I needed to drive to work. It was a short commute. I worked there in Alameda for Del Monte for 22 years. This work was Monday thru Friday. Dee and I attended many Del Monte sponsored festivities while I was employed there: a great place to work, a family-type atmosphere. I have lots of great memories from working there.

Dee continued working as a waitress but she had to work weekends. After some time we decided we wanted our weekends off, to allow Dee and me to do things together. Dee was always so kind and thoughtful, I loved her so much. She stopped working for Wilkinson's because she found a better job working at Ideal Coffee shop, in downtown Oakland, working Monday thru Friday, with weekends off. This was about the time we moved to Oakland, the middle of 1970. At the Ideal Coffee shop, the clientele were mostly office workers, who worked near the restaurant, and only worked Mondays thru Fridays. The first owner was Shirley, a real sweetheart. Dee liked Shirley. But after about a year, Shirley sold the restaurant to a man who wanted it for his wife to operate. His wife was born in Japan. The man said he wanted something for his wife to do. The wife was great, but the man, not very nice. Dee worked with the wife for about two years, but then the owner sold the restaurant to another owner, who made it a cafeteria-style eatery. Dee lost her job.

But Dee lucked out: the restaurant up the street needed a

waitress, Mondays thru Fridays. It was owned by a Greek man and his wife. Dee liked working there too; and, of course, acquired many friends. It was a great restaurant, it had really good food. The burgers were really popular, and the fries too. They served breakfast, but the lunch crowd was the biggest clientele. Many office and retail salespeople came to eat there. It was very close to the Oakland Tribune Building, and several of those workers also came in to eat. But one day, the owner's wife, who also worked there as a waitress, and another employee, accused Dee of doing something wrong to a customer. Dee had been working there for over a year, and had been a waitress for numerous years. As a result, the owner fired Dee. I could not understand this, or why, or what happened. Dee had been working there for some time and had never had any complaints about her work. Dee was very upset because she liked working there. She had never been fired from any job before. I never knew exactly what the error was, but sometime later, Dee finally told me the other waitress caused the problem. The other waitress lied about what happened and blamed it on Dee. I wanted to get it straightened out, but Dee would not let me get involved. I respected Dee, but I felt so sorry for her because she was extremely upset. I knew that what happened did not have anything to do with Dee. She was fired for a mistake made by another employee, who placed the blame on her. Dee would never mistreat customers. I knew the owner somewhat, and I am sure he and I could have gotten the whole thing straightened out. The owner was a kind man, and I think the blame fell on the wrong person. Even with Dee never working there again, I felt the situation should have been cleared up, so no one would have hard feelings. And as it turned out, the owner went to the same church that we attended. We used to talk with the restaurant owner at church, but we never brought up the firing subject. No need to bring up the past. The man was always kind to us, we liked him. But the wife was not kind to anyone. The wife is the one who made the owner fire Dee. She was wrong, but would never admit it. It could have been the owner's wife who made the mistake at this restaurant. I often wondered if some sort of jealousy created this problem.

After Dee was fired, she worked at a different cafeteria-style restaurant for a couple of months, over on Broadway. It was a tough place to work. Luckily, another local restaurant, Fulton Lunch, in the same area, needed a waitress. Dee applied and they welcomed her with open arms. The Fulton Lunch loved Dee. Dee brought some new customers to the new place. The Fulton Lunch owner knew the Greek man, owner of the restaurant who fired Dee. He told him that firing Dee was the best thing he ever did. Dee helped the Fulton Lunch business grow. The Fulton Lunch owner lived pretty close to us and soon gave Dee a key, to allow her to get in and prepare for the day ahead. I would take Dee to work early, go in with her, and lock her in until the owner came a short time later. Then I would go back home, and work on my Architecture course, before going to Del Monte. Dee would get things ready for the day ahead. The owner and his wife ran the restaurant, along with a couple other employees. They were all nice people, and after a while, we began socializing with them. It started mostly by eating out, they liked dinner houses. Dee worked there for about 5 years but got tired of some of the negative happenings among the workers. The owner's wife was also a waitress, and there was one other waitress, three altogether, counting Dee at this restaurant. The owner's wife and the other waitress were always arguing about something. Little no matter things, but they had become very large to them. And this negativity radiated on the other workers, including Dee. It was sad they could not get their differences worked out. Dee and I talked about this extensively. We just could not see anything positive working out. So I advised Dee to quit. The owner and his wife had talked about selling the restaurant anyway. Chinese-owned restaurants were popping up everywhere, and there was a lot of competition between restaurants in the area, while office workers in downtown Oakland were becoming fewer and fewer. The owner asked Dee and me to buy the restaurant. Things were changing too much in downtown Oakland. We both talked about it, but in the end it was an easy decision: we said no. Dee was ready for a change but we could not see any future owning a restaurant. At that time, restaurants were becoming very competitive, profit margins were shrinking, clientele was shrinking, and some fast food restaurants were moving in. Sit down breakfast/lunch restaurants, mostly, were slowly dying because of the loss of local shopping, and loss of office workers. I continued to work at Del Monte, with a steady paycheck to support us, and I was also taking a home study Architecture course. Now that the years have passed, our decision worked out for the better. Whenever a person changes their occupation, there is no guarantee the change will work out. But this change worked out well for Dee. And it helped our future, by having similar working hours. And we usually had the weekends off. This allowed us time to do many of the things we wished to do. It was a good move for both of us.

    When Dee was working as a waitress, she would wash her uniform each evening after work, and let it dry. She said she wanted to wash out the food smell. Dee's uniforms were made of nylon, and they dried fairly fast. But at that time, we only had a floor furnace in our house. Dee would hang her uniform over the furnace to help it dry quicker. And then she would iron it each morning before work. Dee did this routine for years. I wanted her to buy more uniforms, and she did purchase one, but she wanted to clean her uniforms this way. Dee used aprons, and she had several pretty ones. At some point, we purchased a washing machine. We did not have a dryer but hung the wet clothes outside on the clothesline, or inside the house on lines, and clothes drying racks.

Over the years, we had to replace washing machines, but this routine for drying our clothes continued for fifty plus years. Recently, in 2018, a friend told me about compact washing and drying machines. By this time I was doing all the washing of clothes. I measured our house and found the amount of space needed to put in a new compact washer and dryer. It required a small modification of the area where I wanted it. After looking on the computer, and using their measurements, and going to the store to make sure they would fit, I purchased a new compact washer and dryer. What wonderful products these are. So very helpful. I only wish I would have thought about investigating this many years ago. It could have made it so much easier for Dee to handle the laundry. I did help Dee some with the laundry over the years, but Dee did 90% of it. And I helped Dee with the ironing too. But these modern appliances are so helpful. They have spoiled me. Of course, Dee spoiled me, much too often, by not asking me to help her more. Dee just did not ask! Dee left waitressing in 1976 and after she was hired at Kaiser, in 1977, she only needed to wear regular street clothes. Dee liked the idea of not needing to wear uniforms and we did purchase many new clothes for Dee to wear to work. She always liked wearing sweatshirts, and t-shirts, but they were not appropriate for Medical office work. Dee's old uniforms are hanging in our closets.

Dee and I never argued about money, not from day one. We always had a dish on the cabinet, and we would put our money in it, after payday. If either of us needed money for something, we would go to the dish and take out what we needed. It did not matter for what purpose unless it was for something big, which required saving for. Believe me, Dee knows how to save. But I remember, we were having difficulty saving money. We would save it, put it aside, but then we would need it for something. We tried this for some time, but we continued to be unsuccessful. I thought about how we could save, and then leave it there. I found that Del Monte had a savings investment program. In 1974, I started putting 2% of my hourly wage into the program. About $20 per month at first. I could get the funds out, but it would take some time. This worked out very well, even to this day. We were saving, and it was not hurting us, and we still had our dish. A lot of the time we were living on Dee's salary, and putting my check in the bank for bills. I could also move extra money over to a savings account, which we had started at the bank. We have always used this method for finances since the early 1970s. Our Del Monte savings is steadily growing. This has been a tremendous help for us, especially now that we are retired.

We were doing good, until we moved to the house we rented in Oakland. We moved from the apartment in Alameda because the lady upstairs had mean grandchildren living with her. And we were afraid her grandkids would break in when we were not at home, and injure our kitty, Duchess. All our utilities at this apartment were paid by the apartment owner. After our move, we then acquired bills for utilities, phone, water, etc. I suggested that we start a checking account, and eliminate the need for going to the bank to get money orders to send and pay our bills. We started a checking account at the bank we used. Dee said she was going to take care of the checkbook. I thought it would be a good idea, as Dee's penmanship is so much better than my scribbling. Everything went well for a month or two, but then we received letters asking why some checks were made out for a different utility company's bill. Dee was putting the phone's check in the water company's envelope, the gas company's check in someone else's envelope, etc. Now I loved Dee, but I could see this was not going to work. So to this day, I have always written the checks to pay our bills, etc. I have never had any problems.

The Changes for Dee's Work

Dee quit the restaurant work after 18 years, because we felt Dee needed a change. Dee was always a Union worker and the fact of shrinking Union Waitress work needed in downtown Oakland influenced our decision. Because Dee did not drive, she needed to ride the bus to get to work. That is why Dee wanted to work in downtown Oakland. We had talked extensively about what Dee could do. And I suggested the medical field, as there will always be a need for medical field workers. Then Dee decided to go to Medical Transcription school. This is a course detailing the different parts of the human body, and the different terms the doctors use to identify the different parts. This was a challenging subject. I never knew how Dee found out about this subject. It was a year-long class, here at Dewey High School, which was close to our house. Dee studied very hard. I tried to help her as much as I could, but I was not much help. Dee had many classmates there that she liked, and who liked her. There were 30 adults in the class. Dee passed with a fairly high grade in 1977 and then started looking for work.

Dee remained friends with one of her classmates. This lady had 3 children and became pregnant sometime during that school year. She had a son after they had graduated from the Medical Transcription School, and we became his Godparents. We liked the little guy but lost contact with him and his mother after some time. It has been several years now since the last time we saw them. The mother did contact us and said they had moved to a different city close by. His mother said our godchild wanted to see us. I believe he was about 15 years old at that time. So we went to their apartment, picked him up, ate out, and visited for an afternoon. We then took him back home. We left him with our phone number, address, and asked him to contact us, as we wanted to see how he progressed through the next few years. But that was the last time we saw him, and we have never heard from him since. His mother did run into Dee at the hospital where Dee was working, at a later time. She said they had moved out to the valley, here in California, about 75 miles away. It has been at least 25 years now since we have seen any of them. We liked them, and hope they are all well, and happy. Later in this book, I have more about Dee's employment.

Friends

There was not a lot of need for people with Medical Transcription education. Dee put in her application many places, worked at a couple of places for a day or a week as a temporary worker, but did not like the work there. She did not care for the nursing homes. Dee had no experience in the medical field, only waitresses work, but she kept searching. But luckily, Kaiser Permanente hired her as a temporary worker, working in Central Appointments. That department made appointments for all the Medical doctors. Dee liked it there, but it was a temporary job with no benefits. It was almost full-time because of vacations, personal time off, etc. At Kaiser, people have to bid on jobs. Jobs are awarded by qualifications and seniority. I believe there were about 10 people working in this department at the time.

Dee became close to a few of the Central Appointment employees. She liked everyone, and most people like Dee. Dee stayed in contact with some of them but lost contact with others for various good reasons. One lady sort of adopted Dee. This lady was married and had three children. I never knew exactly how these two ladies, Dee and Maria, became close. But Maria was quite a character. Dee also stayed friends with some of the other employees in Central Appointments, but eventually lost contact with most, because of moving to different departments, marriages, retirements, etc. Some of the children of those lady friends caused complications with their working conditions. And Dee and I tried to help some. We hope they all have been doing well. We do know some have passed on.

Maria wanted Dee to be her daughter's Godmother. That was nice, and Dee felt comfortable doing this. It was a memorable service at their church. Maria somehow had taken some dancing lessons, and she had Dee's Goddaughter (about 5 years old then) enrolled in a dancing school. The school puts on dancing, and singing shows a couple of times each year. It was fun to see these little children doing their thing. I do not know if any of the children became professional dancers. But Maria and her daughter did well, and the other mothers danced well too. It was a fun experience. Many years later, we attended this young lady's wedding, which took place in a very beautiful church, in San Francisco. And now she has three lovely daughters, and a great husband.

Maria's oldest son was always studying. I would see him at Kaiser, waiting for his mother. He always had a book in his hands and frequented the Kaiser Library. He later became a doctor. And how he loved the piano. He was a great piano player. He could have been a concert pianist. But he was a perfectionist. Maybe he took it too seriously. He studied, and became a doctor, then a Cardiologist, at a hospital in another state. He is married and has three sons. We did not attend his wedding. Even though he lives in another state, he has always remained close to all his family. A very nice young man, with a nice family of his own.

Maria's middle son was a track star. We went to some of the events he participated in. He did very well in his events. We learned he had to give it up, because of foot problems, but that did not stop him. He studied hard, worked at his own business for a while and is now a professor at a local college. Maria and her husband asked me to become this son's Godfather. I said I would be honored, and became his Godfather. I cannot remember the exact time period. But he is now married to a wonderful young lady. We attended their wedding at one of the Missions here in California. His wife is a wonderful nurse, at one of the local hospitals. She is so helpful to me. If I have a question or problem with Dee, I call her and get her help and advice. They now have a son and daughter. Another remarkable family.

Maria, her husband and their children were a special family. Maria and her husband seemed to be great teachers to their children. They taught their children common sense, to use their minds, and to do things for the betterment of themselves, and their families and to try to help make this a better world. They were always inviting Dee and me to be included with them doing the family things, along with their family. Dee and I appreciated being a part of their lives. And the children included us in their activities too. Dee and I never had children and this family made us feel a big part of theirs. This whole family and Dee and I did many things together. We shared many meals at many different restaurants over the years. And over the years, Maria's family has always invited Dee and me to their house for Thanksgiving dinner. Some years, the dinner would be on a different day than Thursday, because of other commitments. We have gotten together with this family, for Thanksgiving, for 40+ years. And we have attended many activities with this family: marriages, graduations, births, plus many dinners, and other events, so many of them. This relationship all came about from Kaiser hiring Dee. Somehow, Maria must have seen how sweet a person Dee was, and is. Dee is special to all of us. We all love Dee!! Recently, Maria passed from this world. She was not ill for very long and lost her life suddenly. It has left a big void in many people, her family, brothers, sisters, and so many of her friends. And me too. Dee would be very upset, losing this friend, if Dee knew. May Maria rest in Peace.

Another lady who connected with Dee was Brenda. Brenda also had a young daughter. Dee and I attended some of Brenda's daughter's activities over the years. Some were when the daughter was young, maybe 6ish. Other activities were when she was a little older. And of course, we attended the daughter's graduation and wedding. The wedding was at a very cute little church and was a very memorable occasion. Brenda and Dee used to love to get together at numerous parties, which the Kaiser doctors sponsored. One special one was Brenda's mother's retirement party. We have also kept in contact with Brenda, since retirement. We have eaten together at restaurants on occasions. Dee and Brenda loved to go to Bingo games. I understand they had some fond memories of some of these games. I do not think they were ever asked to leave the game!! Sadly, Brenda's mother recently passed. Dee also knew her mother from Kaiser. May she rest in Peace. Brenda occasionally stops by our house to visit Dee and me. We love Brenda and wish her, and her daughter the best in their futures.

Another lady was Mary, with whom Dee has remained friends. Mary also had three children. We never knew much about Mary's two daughters, only their names and ages. But Mary's son and I connected. His father died when he was young. I have tried to include him in a few things, he is a good person. I was able to take him to a few Oakland Raider football games. We attended his marriage, some of his daughter's birthday parties, and a few other activities over the years. This son is one of our executors for Dee's and my estate. Mary and her husband used to get together with us for breakfast. Several times, her son would also eat with us. We are unable to get together now, because of Dee's condition. But I do remember all these wonderful friendships of Dee's.

One of the therapists who Dee worked with at Kaiser was Kathy. The one big thing they had in common was they both liked kitties. And both of them had kitties of their own. I think all kitties were rescue kitties. I know Dee's were. But Kathy was always energetic, at most all the doctor's parties over the years. And Kathy had a big influence over Dee's retirement party. Kathy retired from Kaiser but remained working as a therapist on her own and Kathy has always remained close to Dee. She comes to visit ever so often. Kathy used to eat out with us at times. She is a good person and a good friend to both Dee and myself. For sure, most of our friends have come through Dee. I have only stayed in contact with old high school, and Navy friends. Dee is a big asset to me, and our society. Dee is special.

Another lady whom Dee connected with was Carol. Carol also has a daughter, and when the daughter came here, we laughed a lot.The daughter lives in another state now. We had lots of fun playing card games. Dee met Carol at Kaiser, about 1980. Carol has remained a very close friend for Dee and me, since the time they met each other. To this day, Carol comes to watch Dee for me when I need to run errands, because I never want to leave Dee alone. I go to the garage for a few minutes at a time, but I come in and check on Dee every 15 minutes. Carol lives close by, and is truly a person we can count on for needed help. Carol visited Dee when Dee was in the hospital. Carol frequently brings food for all of us to share. We three used to eat out at several restaurants in the past, sadly some of which have now closed. Carol, who is also retired, loves baseball and has taken Dee and me to a few A's ball games here at the Oakland Coliseum.

Dee's working at Kaiser

After Dee was hired and worked at Kaiser's Central Appointment Department for a few months, there was an opening in the General Medical Clinic. Dee was qualified for the receptionist position. This required her to be on call. Dee could ride the bus to work if Kaiser called, but I was able to take her to work for an early shift and I would pick her up after the shift. If they wanted her to come in the next day, they usually would tell her when to come in. It was better this way, then Dee knew exactly when to be at work. But Dee was getting closer to a full-time employee. If a person had worked at Kaiser for 6 months, they automatically became a full-time employee. I don't think Kaiser called Dee more than a couple of times to come in before she became a full-time employee. After a couple months in the Medical Clinic, Dee was assigned to be the receptionist in the Emergency Department, on the 2nd shift. This certainly was a good experience for anyone, to see so many sick and injured people coming in to get help. It was usually quite busy. She only had to work in the Emergency Room for about 6 months. Dee was still a temporary employee when she was assigned to the Emergency Room Department at first, but became a full-time employee while assigned there. Now Dee had full benefits. But it was not very long, a few months, until Dee was assigned back to the Medical Clinic. After Dee had been assigned to this department for about 2 years, there became a need for a receptionist in the Psychiatry Department.

Dee was not very happy to go to the Psychiatry Department. Having very little seniority, Dee was pretty much drafted. It all worked out though, because the doctors liked Dee, Dee liked the doctors and the patients and she wanted to help. As time went by the department expanded and moved to different locations. Afterward things settled down, and Dee, being a workhorse, did well. People went to her for help to answer their questions. Dee was always a conscientious and responsible person who would always put the other person first and she ended up working in the Psychiatry Department for 24 years. All the doctors and patients liked Dee, everyone liked Dee. And the Psychiatry staff liked to party a lot. Someone was always celebrating something. Because Dee did not drive, I always took her to their get-togethers, so I was usually invited. These celebrations were celebrated at many different locations. Lots of fun, and plenty of food and drink. I enjoyed talking to some of the doctors about architecture, the lottery, a little of everything that may have been in the current news. Dee received several awards, but never took any of them too seriously. Once, when Frank was the head doctor of the department, he came into the reception area, and asked Dee how she was doing. Dee replied: "What's it to ya?' Dee and Frank were always teasing each other. Frank would have been in serious trouble if the "Me-too" movement was around at that time. So to make laughs out of it, the reception staff made t-shirts for each receptionist, with "What's it to Ya" on them. I do not know how long this went on. The work got done, and there were always plenty of laughs. And many days, while Dee worked there she registered over 100 patients a day, that's a lot! At the end of the workday, Dee's cash and checks had to balance with the records. Some days Dee had to stay a half-hour or more, to correct some discrepancy. Any money problems had to be worked out before Dee could go home. Days like this, Dee would be tired, maybe a little frustrated too. This would definitely be a night to eat out!

At times, Dee would bake things and take them to work to share with everyone. At one time while working in the Psychiatry Department, someone came up with an idea for a food competition. Dee entered with a salad called Psychotic Break Salad. Dee won the competition, the salad was good, but the name was better. The salad was something like cottage cheese on the bottom, lime jello in the middle, and Cool Whip on top. Dee could come up with wonderful ideas.

Dee retired after 26 years working at Kaiser Permanente in 2004. Many things happened during her employment there, lots of fun, and lots of memories. Dee had the brainpower to understand things, explain things, and explain with accuracy. Just knowing Dee, a great mind, a great person, I think Dee would have made a wonderful school teacher.

Dee's Health

Dee's health has gone through many stages over the years. In 1994, Dee had back problems, lots of pain. The doctor gave Dee an epidural, which lasted about a year. An epidural is a shot of steroids, injected into the spine. But then the back pain came back, later in 1995. The Kaiser doctor gave Dee another epidural, but this time Dee ended up with a drop foot on her left side. It has caused many problems, up to this current date. We later heard that the wrong size needle was used, severing the nerve, or crushing it, causing the drop foot. The problem with the foot, we were told, the drop foot problem would wear off and go away after 6 months. But that did not happen, and she still has the drop foot . It causes her to trip a lot. I always walked hand in hand with her, to catch her if she were to fall. And Dee has fallen too many times. Way too many times!

Then in November of 1996, Dee had an aneurysm on the lower part of her brain, just above her right eye. She was at home, and experienced tremendous headache pain. I took her to Kaiser ER in Oakland. They transferred her to Kaiser in Redwood City. Redwood City Kaiser did the surgery, they had to remove a small piece of her skull, and put a clip on the leaking vein. This was a scare. The doctor said Dee could end up blind, or could be paralyzed. Immediately after the surgery, the doctor came and told me, as Dee was coming out of anesthesia, everything works. This doctor was so very happy, he was dancing. That relieved me and really made me happy too. Dee recovered well, and has had no problems since that time. We sincerely thank the Medical Staff at Kaiser Redwood City.

In June of 1998, Dee was chasing the kitty when she slipped on the rug and broke her left ankle.. This required surgery, and a metal plate with screws. Dee was supposed to walk on crutches, a very tough thing for Dee to do, for about a month. Never being too well-coordinated, using crutches presented problems for her.

In February of 2000, Dee stepped on her untied shoelace, and fell and broke her left hip. When this happened she was out in our garage but managed to get our neighbor's attention. I was not home, I was out golfing. The break required surgery and metal pins were inserted to hold everything in place. Poor girl! I had come home and was at the hospital when the surgeon talked to me before the surgery. The surgical team: the surgeon was male, and everyone else on the team was female. I believe there were 7 members on the team. I thought Dee deserved a great team. Again, Dee was told to use crutches. Kaiser has always been so good to Dee and myself. We thank the Medical team at Kaiser Oakland also.

More recently, in August of 2012, due to dehydration, Dee fainted in church. She fell, and broke her backbone in many places. Her butt hit the pew as she was falling. No surgery was needed, but some vertebrae in her back are pretty much gone. Dee had a lot of pain for a while, but that finally went away. Every once in a while she complains, but only for a moment or two. I have seen the x-rays and I am surprised she does not have a lot of pain now. When I get her out of bed is when she complains most. It probably straightens the backbone and puts pressure on the bad disks. Now in July of 2020 she twisted her right foot, and broke her right ankle, which did require surgery. More pins were inserted to stabilize the foot. But this time, she did not need to use crutches. She would not have been able to use them anyway. Instead, they put a walking boot on her foot to wear, for a short time. Poor girl has a lot of metal in her body and broken bones. She was diagnosed a long time ago with Osteoporosis. This surgery was also done at Kaiser Oakland. Again, we thank the Medical Staff.

The Monterey Area

Dee and I liked to go to Monterey, and Carmel California. Dee especially liked it there. There is so much to do there, and pretty much within walking distance. They both have lots of restaurants, shops, museums, and much more, not to mention the beach areas. In the '80s and '90s, we probably went there about every other weekend, and sometimes every weekend. There are just so many things to investigate, for tourists like us. And the whole area is pretty safe, we never heard of any robbery or that type of problem. We would sometimes go down on Friday night, stay over two nights, and then I would come home Sunday by myself. I would work the following week, care for our cats in the morning and night too. Then I would go back to Monterey the following Friday night after work. Dee enjoyed being there by herself, to read, relax, shop, and look in all the stores. Then she would tell me about the restaurants she had searched out, and wanted us to try. Dee liked her private time alone. Dee would sometimes write our Christmas cards while there. The one motel where we stayed regularly in Monterey, (Carmel was too expensive) had our phone number. They would call us and give us the best room available for that weekend. We did not even need to check in on Friday nights. They would put the key in a certain location for us to get when we did arrive, no matter the time. This was great because getting there by closing time was difficult sometimes. Sometimes we did not get out of work on time, traffic could be horrendous, etc. One time, it took me two hours just to get to San Jose, normally a 45 minute drive. But the motel knew we were good customers, and we always paid with no hesitation. Plus they only had a hot tub, no pool and that meant there would be fewer kids staying there. We learned the layout of Monterey like going out to our backyard. Dee and I were able to really relax. I am so happy Dee liked Monterey so much. It was like I was giving her a real treat. Because Dee did not drive, and I loved this girl, I wanted to give Dee as much as I could. Dee deserved her private, relaxation time. Plus I could call Dee in her room, in the evenings. Because caring all the time for our kitties, and my work, I felt good about letting Dee have a break. I usually did not stay for the week. Because I wanted Dee to have her own time to relax, and do just whatever she wanted to do. At that time in our working career, Dee had more time off from work than I did. Dee was very good at investigating different things to look at and do when I did get there. It was a very safe area. This wonderful Catholic church is only about 3 blocks down the hill, and Dee loved to go to Daily Masses. Of course, we went to Daily Masses here in Oakland too. But during the time Dee spent there by herself, she would tell me about some of the most interesting things about the area she had discovered. There is a lot of history from way, way back, concerning that whole area. There are many fabulous restaurants to eat at, in downtown Monterey. We patronized many of them, and we discovered which menu items we liked best. And bakeries! There are some wonderful pastry products produced, and we found the ones we thought were the best. Many restaurants sit on the ocean and have wonderful views, with seafood items on their menus.

Monterey used to be a fishing town and has a lot of fishing

history. For example, The Monterey Bay Aquarium is so big! Yes, most of it is in the ocean. Monterey Bay is about the same size as the Grand Canyon, but it is filled with ocean water, not air as in the Grand Canyon. At one point, it is about a mile deep. And there are many different kinds of fish, Marine life, otters, sea lions, and so much more to investigate for us tourists. There are college students studying marine life, probably using that knowledge for their future. There are divers and diving schools. It is quite an experience. We always walked along the seashore, around the ocean border, walked on the piers, and just enjoyed ourselves. There is some commercial fishing, lots of boat trips, fishing trips, etc.. I could go on. But Dee and I just loved to sit, watch the birds, the people, kids, dogs, etc.. Monterey has some outdoor shows, close to the pier. There is different entertainment at certain times of the year. Museums are very interesting. Of course, Monterey also has many of the best golf courses in the country. Dee and I spent many hours, many days exploring the many sights. On each trip, we always discovered something new and of interest to us. Dee always seemed to be so very happy. Yes, we looked at buying a house in that area, but the prices were always out of our reach. I have no idea how we could have managed one, but we dreamed. I was always wanting to please Dee with everything I could, within reason. Dee could be a little extravagant! But I love her.

 Pacific Grove is a little town next to Monterey. It is mostly residential, with a small two-block shopping area downtown. It sits along the Pacific Ocean, has beautiful views, and has a poor man's golf course, because it is laid out, similar to the famous Pebble Beach Golf Course. Along one of the main roads, which leads to the beach, is a restaurant called the Fish Wife Restaurant. It may have a different name now. It is a dinner house, but lunch was served there also. The name probably came from a fisherman who started it many years ago. It has a beautiful atmosphere, very open, decorated with fish designs, and has a large fish aquarium inside. It must be one of the favorite eateries for the local people, as it usually gets busy. Most items on the menu are different types of seafood. Being next to Monterey and the ocean, the restaurant probably gets their seafood fresh daily from the fishermen in the area. Dee and I have gone there several times for lunch, and dinner a couple of times. It could be a little pricey. The reason I am mentioning this is, a few years ago, Dee and I would go there for lunch. The lady who seated us was an older lady in her 80's, as she told us. She did not look her age at all. She looked like she had been a movie actress. She said she lived close to this restaurant, and walked there every day. She came to the restaurant each day at lunchtime to seat people, she was not an employee. But she volunteered to seat people, because she was retired, and wanted something to do. She wanted to be around people, she said. She was an attractive woman, and very smart, and well educated. But I cannot remember her name! She told us that she had an interesting career, before she retired She told Dee and I that she used to train actors and actresses, their lines for their roles in the movies they were acting in. She would help them memorize their lines. She mentioned several names, but most of them were from the '40s, and '50s, and 60's movies. There may have been more names of newer people, but the ones she mentioned were like Bogart, Becall, sort of that era. I wish I could remember more of the names she told us. The amazing thing was, she had red hair, similar to Dee's, and she and Dee were about the same size. Dee and I used to sit in the restaurant, look out the windows, eat our food, and just relax. It was one of the stops we usually tried to patronize when we were in the area. As I have said before, Dee and I always found the best restaurants to eat in, no matter where we were. We would recommend this restaurant to anyone, it is good!!

Carmel, California, is next to Monterey, and Pacific Grove, California. It also became famous because of the actors, and actresses, from Hollywood. Most of them came to relax, and golf. The most famous at that time was Bing Crosby, and he sponsored golf tournaments at the Pebble Beach Golf Course. He invited many famous names to golf with him. And most had the funds to live an easy lifestyle. Bob Hope was usually there, and it seems they invited friends whom they wanted to golf and socialize with. And rumors are there were many bets floating around. Carmel is very quaint, and pretty, and has many beautiful art galleries. Lots of shops, and restaurants. Some are very famous. And many cute little shops. A lot of cute cottage-style homes. Very pricey! Dee and I usually did not stay overnight in Carmel. Carmel attracts many tourists during the summer time. It has just so many quaint, different little shops and atmosphere. And lots of beautiful artworks, mostly of ocean-type scenery.

Golf

Dee suggested I try golfing as a sport. I did and became hooked. I had always liked trying different sports, although I never cared much for tennis. So I started golfing in the mid 1980's. Dee has never complained about the amount of time it requires. Maybe she wished she had never suggested playing golf. She said I might like the sport, and I should try it. Dee has always supported me, and allowed me to go to all these different courses. And I have been able to play several beautiful courses here in northern California. At the time, when I started golf, I never thought golf would require so much of my time. I wish I had cut back some, and spent more time at home with Dee. Dee just never complained about the amount of time I spent away from home, playing golf. I almost always went golfing at some place in the area around Monterey. I loved golfing there. One time Dee had saved enough money for me to play the Pebble Beach Course, $400 then. She said this was a gift she wanted to give me. Dee had really put a lot of thought and effort into this gift for me. I appreciated Dee's kindness. I had already played some of the other courses in that area. Pebble Beach was a really great treat, I will never forget the experience. Dee rode in the cart with me. Dee liked the scenery, and her time there. I played with one man from New Jersey, and his wife also rode in a cart with her husband. The other two men were from Oregon, and they walked, and had their own caddy. The wonderful views from the course, the houses, and especially the ocean scenery, were fascinating. It was a lot of money, but I enjoyed it so much, and I know Dee enjoyed riding along in the cart. That was a treat for her too. And golfing and riding along the ocean, all the scenery was fantastic. There are other courses along the ocean there, which I have played. It was a fun place to visit. We investigated many areas around there, even looked at some houses to buy; we could not afford any, but it was fun to look at. We even went there after Dee retired, but because of her health issues we do not travel there anymore.

    When I came home from a golf outing one time, Dee was very upset. I asked what the problem was. Dee told me she had tried to put a can of spoiled tomato sauce down the kitchen sink drain. Because we do not have a garbage disposal, it clogged the drain. It was not a big deal! I just took the drain pipe apart, cleaned the blockage, and put it back together. Then it worked fine. And I asked Dee not to do this again, because we do not have a disposal.. She agreed, she did not know. Dee was happy after I had cleared the drain. And how these old memories make me love this woman!

Some of Dee's Working History

Yes, I met Dee in February, 1967. We were married in September 1967. We went to Indiana in March 1968. We both worked hard there, saved our money, and moved back to California in May 1969. Dee worked at waitress work until the summer of 1976. Because mom-and-pop restaurants were closing, waitress work was harder to find, especially day shift, and week days only, in downtown Oakland. Dee quit the restaurant work, and in 1976 attended Medical Transcription school for one year. Dee graduated and received her certificate in June 1977. Dee then worked at different places as a temporary for a short time, and then Kaiser hired her as a temporary worker, and then permanently. Dee worked in the General Medical Clinic, and then Kaiser moved her to the Psychiatry Dept. where she worked for 24 years. Dee retired from Kaiser in January, 2004. I wanted her to retire because she had started working as a child, at Prudential Insurance Company as a stock runner, when she was only 14 years old. Dee had worked for about 50 years. I thought that was long enough. Dee did not want to retire, she wanted to keep working, but if she worked at Kaiser any longer, she would lose part of her retirement benefits. This Psychiatry position brought a lot of mental stress, and I knew Dee was tired.

I had worked at Del Monte Corporation from September 1969 to July 1991. It was a good place to work. Then Del Monte moved that plant to Stockton, California. Next I worked for one year for a beer distributing company. Then I went to work for the City of Alameda from Oct 1992 to March 2005, when I retired too. I was tired, as I had done pretty heavy physical work most of my working career. I wanted to save my health for our future travels. We never know what the future can bring.

When we came back to California in 1969, we rented an

apartment in Alameda for a little over a year. Then we rented a house in Oakland for 18 months. In August of 1971, we put a bid on this house, but it needed some upgrades. That work took up until December before we could move in. Before moving in, I came and washed all the walls, ceilings, and floors, and did some other clean-up by myself. I did not want Dee to have to do this cleaning work after we moved in, and it was quite extensive. The previous owners smoked. All our furniture came on Dec 29th. We paid $18,950 @ 7% interest for this house. We had put $600 down and financed the remainder. It was a 30-year loan, but I always paid extra each month, and it was paid off in about 20 years. I never liked making payments for anything. And having to pay interest was not good for us!

When we started making our house a home, we loved flea markets. So most of the things in our home were purchased at flea markets. About everything was used. I scraped and finished things, painted some, and determined what was needed, and we would search for it. We ended up with a lot of excesses too. But over these years, we have been able to move many things along to new homes, or the junk pile. We always liked the quality of older things, that is why we have so many older things. Not too much in the antique category. Our house has always been busy, and full of stuff, but pretty well organized. People who walk in for the first time, spend a few minutes looking around, and usually make some kind of comment. But several of the older things have needed to be replaced with new or newer ones. But Dee and I are still here.

Earlier I had mentioned that in 1974, I started putting 2% of my earnings into the Del Monte Savings Investment Plan. And when I left Del Monte, I had to roll over those monies into IRAs. I have made many changes with those funds. But now that we are older, and required to draw out a certain amount each year, that money comes in handy. Even though the funds came out of my check, the money belonged to both of us, not just me. We banked what we could, and lived on Dee's salary most of the time. We never had to want for much, but I always watched how we were doing. We always budgeted, and now I use some of these monies to make improvements to this house.

Travel

We have always enjoyed each other's company. We never argued. We ate out a lot, and always talked about each other's problems. We talked over things we wanted to do, made plans, etc. We talked about traveling to Europe. We loved traveling, but never went far, mostly to the Carmel and Monterey area, but also to Reno, Nevada, and a few side trips, none of any distance. We went to Monterey almost every weekend. I would golf sometimes, Dee would wander around window shopping, and then we would meet up for lunch or dinner, depending on the time of day. We always went to the shopping center, Cannery Row and just looked around. For a couple of years, we did all our Christmas shopping there. We looked at buying a house in that area, but the prices were always out of our reach. I have no idea how we could have managed one, but we dreamed! I was always wanting to please Dee with everything I could, within reason! Dee could be a little extravagant! But I love her! (This, I had mentioned earlier)

We went to Reno several times. One time around Christmas in the early eighties, we ended up buying a timeshare in Sparks, Nevada just a few short miles from downtown Reno. We tried to use it each year, but we could not coordinate our times. And the place had unusual reservation requirements. Over all the years we owned it, I think we were able to use it about four times. We finally sold it in 2014, as it was a bad investment because we just could not use it. But it was a nice place. We had about $15,000 in it, $5,000 to buy it, and we had to pay another

$3,500 to sell it. And the place was costing us over $600 a year, just to pay maintenance fees, and taxes. A very costly investment!!!

We liked going anywhere! We liked going to Sacramento, California. The problem was, Dee cannot take the heat very well, because of her light skin color. She can easily become overheated if she is in the sun, or extreme heat and cannot get cooler relief close by. Sacramento, California becomes very hot during the summer season, but it is the Capital of California and has a lot of history. It was [a big factor]to gold miners, and prospectors, back in the gold rush days, around 1848. It has lots of big trees, several park-like areas, which allow for people to relax and try to stay cool. The heat did not bother me, but I learned early in our marriage about Dee's getting sick from too much heat. It is a scary thing to see, and much worse, when you know it is your loved one suffering. If the two of us went there to look around, we usually went when the cooler seasons were around. If we went there in the summertime, I may have driven, but we stayed in a hotel, and only went out in the morning or evening. We spent most of our day in air-conditioned places, such as museums, galleries, and sometimes inside the Capitol building itself. And a few times, we rode the air-conditioned amtrak train to Old Town Sacramento and wandered from store to store. But I always tried to watch out for Dee, and my heat concerns for her. One time, in the fall of the year, we stayed a whole week in a little cottage-style place. It was close to the freeway, but the noise did not bother us. It was so cute and relaxing. It had several cottages, but only one or two were occupied at the time we were there. It had a path all around in a circular form, and we could keep walking that path as much as we wanted. We would get out early in the morning and walk, and then find something to eat. We always found good places to eat and we never went hungry. We rarely ate at fast food places, unless they were convenient to the freeway, and then it was usually just for a bathroom break and a cup of coffee. We had two McDonald's which we usually stopped on our way to Reno. But if we were going to Reno to stay overnight, we usually ate at the truck stop in Sacramento. It was about the same if we were going to Monterey. We would stop in Gilroy, California, at McDonald's for our bathroom break, and coffee to take with us. My goodness, it is so good, thinking about all these travels Dee and I have done! And how I wish we could do them all again, so many wonderful memories. When we drove anywhere, of any distance, I always looked at the maps, and made stopping points for bathroom breaks, and coffee, and food breaks. I almost always tried to stop after around 100 miles of driving. If we were going to southern California, we would stop somewhere after driving for two hours. Then we would drive for another 2 hours and stop for another break. Oh, how I wish Dee and I could travel together again.

Children

Early in our marriage, Dee and I talked about having children. We discussed the subject a lot, for a couple of years. Our conclusion was not to have any. Some of the reasons were, we did not feel this was a good neighborhood to raise children. We were wrong about the neighborhood, this is a good neighborhood. Area public schools were not the greatest, but okay. I did not know anything about the Catholic schools. Dee liked her work, I had been at Del Monte for quite a while, studying architecture, and I hoped to become an architect. We had no family here. We had bought this house and had some other goals. It just did not seem like we should have any children. Dee would have made a good mother. At that time, I never thought about Dee acquiring Alzheimer's disease. Now, I am thankful we did not have any children.

Dee's Earlier Years.

Crooked toes. Dee has always had trouble with her feet. When she lived with her step-mother, the step-mother made Dee wear shoes that were too small. Dee lived with the step-mother for about 4 1/2 years. When Dee ran away from her step-mother at age 13, she ran away to her Aunt Marion's house there in Scranton, Pennsylvania. Dee said it was early one morning, around 2 or 3 am. Dee never said anything about the time of year. The step-mother had made Dee wear dirty/filthy clothes, probably hand me downs from someone, or charities. Dee had to wear old shoes the step-mother found for her, which were usually too small, along with the shabby clothes. Dee said the step-mother purchased clothing at thrift stores. When Dee arrived at Aunt Marion's house, Aunt Marion would not let Dee inside, until she took all her clothes off outside. Probably afraid of lice. It seems the step-mother did not like Dee at all, maybe jealousy. Probably because Dee was pretty, fair skin, beautiful hair, a true Irish look, and the fact that Dee was not her child. The step-mother was considered black Irish, with dark eyes and black hair, and she was not so pretty and had a rough personality. Especially with Dee. While Dee lived with the step-mother, Dee's father was an ambassador for the United States in Japan. He was out of the States for 2 years at a time. When he came home, the step-mother would have another child (2 boys), that is all Dee told me about. As Dee's feet grew, she grew out of shoes quickly. She was always asking for new shoes, as the old ones were worn and much too small. So John (Dee's father), jokingly said: "just put the boxes on her feet". Dee did not understand and began crying. Dee thought she would have to wear boxes on her feet to school and church. I suppose he finally explained, but Dee was under a lot of stress while living with the step-mother. And the step-mother would make up lies about Dee, and tell John. Dee would get a spanking, and punishment. from John, because of the lies. To this day, Dee has trouble with her feet.

While Dee lived with the step-mother, there was not much money, while John was out of the country. So the step-mother would spend money on makeup accessories. She always went out dancing on the weekends. And for weeks and months, all Dee had to eat 3 times a day was lima beans. Dee will not eat lima beans now. She suffered malnutrition during those years. Dee has white streaks on her tongue, the signs of malnutrition. Dee must not have had any milk to drink during those years. Dee suffered from bad teeth while living with the step-mother, and while living with her Aunt in New Jersey, and after we were married. The dentist in New Jersey tried to care for Dee's teeth but said they were just too soft. The dentist said Dee's teeth should be pulled, but he would not pull them, because of Dee being so young, at age 14. So the dentist kept putting fillings in Dee's teeth. Dee told me she had 3 and 4 fillings in many of her teeth. The Nuns at Catholic School knew of the mistreatment by the step-mother, but from fear, Dee would never say anything bad about the step-mother because she had threatened that if Dee said anything, Dee's father would get in trouble. The Nuns begged the school to do something, but because Dee's lips were so tightly sealed by a threat from the step-mother, the church could not step in and investigate. It must have been a terrible existence. Improper food, dirty clothes, the threat of being beaten, and then the kids at school made fun of her, especially because of her red hair. And at some time, while living with the step-mother, Dee acquired a head full of lice. I am not sure of Dee's age, but Dee said combing them out really hurt, and pulled her hair. Dee probably got them, because of the dirty living conditions.

Before Dee went to live with her step-mother, Dee's Lithuanian grandmother would fix Dee's hair to look like Shirley Temple's curly hair, back when Shirley Temple was a little girl actress. Along about this time in Dee's life, she was wandering around in a shed out behind the house. On a shelf there was a can of orange paint and somehow that can of paint must not have had a lid on it, and of course, it fell on Dee's head, and paint went all over her hair. The grandmother could not get the paint out of Dee's hair, she had to cut all of Dee's curly red hair off. Dee said her grandmother cried tears for days about this incident. Dee's father and the rest of the family were very upset, but it finally grew back. Dee was the first grandchild of the Palaskas/Pallard family. Dee's father's name at birth was Palaskas, but John could not find a job, because of the prejudice against the Lithuanian people. So he changed his name legally to Pallard. And of course, Dee was born a Pallard. Dee's Aunt Marion was still a teenager at home when Dee was a little girl. Dee and Aunt Marion did many things together before Aunt Marion decided to get married. Dee's favorite was Aunt Marion. And another thing about Dee's grandmother, Marcella. When Dee was just a little girl, when Marcella was caring for her, Marcella must have drank quite large amounts of coffee. Dee said Marcella had a pot of coffee on the stove all the time. Marcella would get a cup of milk for Dee, and then put a few drops of coffee in it. This made Dee so happy!! Marcella said Dee was a grown-up person now because she was drinking coffee. And Dee thought she was a grown-up person now, being able to drink coffee even though it was only a few drops in the milk. And when John came home from work, Dee would run to him, exclaiming about how she was a grown-up girl and was drinking coffee just like grownups. Dee was so excited about the coffee. How well Dee remembered the details about the coffee, very exactly. And to this day, Dee loves her coffee!! Dee loved her grandmother Marcella, and Marcella begged Dee's father, John, to let Dee stay with Marcella after Dee's mother died. John would not let Dee stay, he said that Marcella was not too well balanced, this was his excuse. Then John made Dee go to live with the step-mother.

    Another story Dee told me about her family. Once Dee had reached the right age, she was going to attend the Holy Rosary School next to the Catholic Church. Aunt Marion asked John if he had made any arrangements for Dee's first day at school. John said no, Dee could go there by herself. He asked Dee if she knew the way to the school and if she could make it there by herself. Dee responded, yes, she knew her way to the school, and where it was. John said Dee knew the way, and again said Dee could go by herself. Aunt Marion argued with John, saying that he should take his daughter to her first day at school. John said no, she knows the way and said again, she can go by herself. Well, Aunt Marion did not agree, and Aunt Marion took Dee to her first day at school. That was good, because when they arrived at the school many kids were crying and sobbing and did not want to go into the school, nor leave their mothers. Dee became a little scared and asked Aunt Marion, "What are they going to do to us?" Dee thought, from the appearance, that something bad was going to happen to all of them. She wanted to know what punishment was going to happen to them. Aunt Marion said to Dee, "The children do not want to leave their mothers or family for the whole day at school". Dee said "Oh, OK" and away Dee went, no longer frightened. Dee was happy to go to school and liked learning. Her only problem was, her family only spoke the Lithuanian language at home. As a result, Dee did not know much English language. But after a few days, Dee was in the full swing of things. Dee liked school and kindergarten. I am sure Aunt Marion tried to teach Dee some English language too. And Dee said John used to sing songs to her in the English language.

Some of Dee's History

Over our years of marriage, Dee never wanted to go back to see her birthplace and the area where she lived as a young child. I asked her many, many times, and she always said no. I always wanted Dee to have the opportunity to visit her birthplace, and any memories she may have had. I was curious to see her first home and see all the things she had told me about over the years. I truly wanted her to visit her birthplace if she wanted to. The things she told me about, the hotel-type house, church, school, the dump that she played at, even though she was not supposed to go there. I wanted to meet any of her family, but none of the family lives there now. The store where her father worked (Noon's Grocery) is there today. I never knew where Dee's Aunt Marion lived, but it was in Scranton, Pennsylvania, close to the church and school. I did find where her Hennigan grandparents lived, but it was not close to Dee's home. I never found out where the step-mother lived, while Dee lived with her. But I know it was also close to the school, only a couple blocks, and not far from Dee's grandmother's house by the church. Dee only lived about 2 blocks from the church, and the school was next door to the church. This is where Dee developed her strong Catholic Faith. Dee was alone and felt abandoned sometimes, and therefore Dee counted on her God to help her. Of course, the Nuns wanted to help Dee at different times, but Dee would just not let them, as she was terrified of the step-mother. But more so, Dee loved her father dearly and did not want to cause him any grief. Of course, the step-mother told Dee's father many lies about Dee, and Dee would get punished. Dee would never fight with anyone, and Dee would never fink on anyone, no matter what may have been the reason. And the step-mother knew Dee would never tell, for fear of getting her father into trouble.

While Dee lived with the step-mother, the step-mother became pregnant. She had 2 sons that Dee told me about. Bootsie was one. When the step-mother went out on Saturday night, Dee had to babysit. These two boys must have been infants or very young. Dee was to feed them, change them, etc. But if they messed in their pants, or caused any stress or trouble, Dee would get hit and beaten, when the step-mother came home. Then the step-mother would lie to John about what happened. Dee had to wear sweaters, and long sleeves to school to cover the bruises on her arms and body. The step-mother must have liked to punish Dee. The Nuns at the school suspected the abuse, but the step-mother had put so much fear in Dee, that Dee would never tell the school how she acquired the injuries.

Through the years, Dee has told me about her childhood, about where she was raised. Dee told me the story about her mother, father, and family before she went to live with the step-mother. Dee's mother went to the County Mental Hospital when Dee was 1 year old. Dee never saw her biological mother alive. The only time Dee saw her biological mother was after she had died, and was in her casket. The reason Dee's mother (Mary) ended up in a mental hospital was, when Dee's mother was 9 years old, she had gone down to the rail yard to meet her father (Hennigan), who worked as a switchman for the railroad. This was the end of the day, and his shift was over, and time for him to go home. As Dee explained it, when the father saw his daughter, he started running toward her. But he did not see the train coming, and he was hit by the train and killed. Dee's mother witnessed this, and never could get over what she had seen, a terrible experience! And to make things worse, Dee's (Hennigan)grandmother blamed Dee's mother for his death. Later Dee's grandmother apologized, but that did no good. All the damage had already been done. But after Dee's mother gave birth to Dee, and Dee was growing, the doctors said that the trauma Mary had experienced earlier in her life, had caused her mind to crumble, and therefore she needed to be placed in a mental hospital. So Dee's mother lived in the hospital for 6 years, until she died of tuberculosis, in 1945. Dee was never taken to the hospital to see her mother. Dee only saw her biological mother in her casket. Dee could only remember the pretty pink dress her mother had on in her casket. Seemed so sad to me.

After Dee's birth, Dee lived in an old rooming hotel rented by her grandfather, (Peter Palaskas). Her grandmother (Marcella Palaskas, John's mother) raised Dee until Dee had to go live with the step-mother, at seven years old. This house was the family home for the Palaskas family, the mother, father, (a coal miner), 4 daughters, and 2 sons. Patricia was the oldest girl, and John, Dee's father, was the oldest of all the children. The grandmother was not well balanced, as she had hormonal issues early in life. Dee said her grandmother, Marcella, had a nervous breakdown at age 39 and refused to leave the house. She would go as far as the lawn and that was it. Later when she had to move, they had to remove her in a straight jacket.

Dee's grandfather (Peter Palaskas) worked in the coal mines most of his life. After he left mining work and retired, he took a position at the Hillside County Home. He cared for the livestock there, milked the cows, etc. The Home had other workers to handle the other maintenance. He lived there during the week and came home on the weekends. Then Marcella would wash his clothes, and ready them for the next week. The grandfather, Pete, was always a laborer and considered poor. Peter Palaskas had very little education and must have been a teenager when he came to the United States from Lithuania. Dee's grandfather came to this country from Lithuania for a better life. The grandmother had come from a farm in Lithuania. She was known as wealthy, and country, because of her upbringing and just like many others, she wanted to make a better life for herself and her family. Marcella Palaskas must also have been in her early 20's, maybe late teens, when she came to the United States. The grandmother had come to Pennsylvania, originally to help her sister with the sister's pregnancy and her family. The sister's husband worked here. Dee never said what he did, and Dee may not have even known. But shortly after Marcella arrived here, her sister and her immediate family moved back to Lithuania. Marcella could not move back to Europe with them, because she had no money, or a job to get the money. She was stuck here with no money. She knew no one and did not speak any English. Then she connected with Peter, the grandfather, and they married, made a home, and started a family with John, Dee's father, being the firstborn. John was born in 1911. Then five more children came along. I think Peter Palaskus was born in 1886, and Marcella Palalskus. was born in 1889.

Marcella was a housewife. She was given all the money from Pete, to supply the needs for the family. Marcella was very frugal. She saved all the newspapers, saved all the cans, washed them, flattened them, and stored everything very neatly in the basement of the house. This was about the time of the Great Depression, when metal and paper was saved by all households. It was never clear to me as to why she saved things like these, but metal and paper was also collected for the WWII effort. If I remember correctly, the government needed the metal to build tanks and airplanes for the war effort. Marcella did all her shopping at the Huckster wagon, which came along once a week. The Huckster wagon was a wagon holding fresh produce, and other household supplies. It was pulled by a horse. I remember other people talking about buying many very useful things from the Huckster wagon. Marcella was very clean. She washed all the dishes twice after eating. She would also pour boiling water over the dishes as a rinse, two times, after every meal. Dee told me Marcella washed all the clothes in a large tub. Marcella washed all sheets by hand, and boiled the water for rinsing the sheets. All the water was heated on the stove. She used a stick to remove the sheets from the tub, and the clothing, and hung them on a line. Marcella used lye soap for washing the clothes and sheets. The clothesline must have been in the backyard. Dee said Marcella used a wheel with a rope on it, for putting the wet clothes out. The house had a huge old iron cook stove for all the heating of the house, and cooking. She probably burnt coal in the stove. Dee had a chair behind the stove, to help stay warm in the winter time. Sometimes Marcella and Dee would sit on chairs, and put their feet in the stove oven to warm their feet during cold winter days. Marcella had the old steel irons, Potts Irons, that were used at that time for ironing, and Marcella would place them in Dee's bed before Dee went to bed for the night, to prewarm the bed for her. If you do not know about the irons, they were like a heavy oval cast iron piece of metal, with no handle but with a slot on top to attach a handle. The handle could be attached to an iron for ironing, and as that iron became cooler, Marcella could put it back on the stove for reheating, and then attach the handle to a different iron to continue ironing. Most households had 3 or 4 of these irons. My mother used them, and my grandparents had three. I relate to this, as when I was born, our house used the old iron cook stove for heat and cooking. My parents' home, when I was an infant, had no electricity at that time, but Dee said Scranton and their house had electricity when she was born. Dee said Marcella had a vegetable and flower garden in the back.

When Dee was born, John worked at the grocery store in front of their house, (Noon's Grocery). John must have helped with some of the household expenses, while working at this store. John later became manager of this store. Dee was allowed to go to this store to buy things for Marcella. Marcella had an ongoing charge account, and would pay her bill at the end of the week.

John went to church with Dee and his mother on Sundays. Peter did not go with them. After church, they would stop and buy donuts on their way home. I think the grocery must have sold donuts, because it was never clear where the donut shop was. Dee said that was a big treat for the entire family. I think the family was a happy family, because Pete would play tricks on his children, and tease them. He used to put coffee in his spoon, and then, unaware to the receiver, he would flip the spoon, and the coffee would hit the target child on the forehead. And of course that would start the ruckus! Pete loved doing this, and you never knew when it was coming. Dee was targeted many times. All the kids liked this game. Dee said Marcella would bounce up and down while laughing! I imagine they made some pretty good messes to clean up. The house had a huge kitchen, and a kitchen table. The kitchen table was big, round, and could easily seat ten people. Dee said the kitchen had lots of chairs. This house was a rooming house for miners, before Pete moved his family in. The whole family spoke only Lithuanian language. Dee told me a few Lithuanian words when we were first married, but I have forgotten them. The slang frog word was the most popular, - Tiputa chae??

Of the money Pete gave to Marcella, to run the household: after they had been married 20 years, Marcella managed to save $2,000 over those years. Marcella had kept the money hidden in a glass jar, in her secret location. Pete knew nothing about what she had been doing. Then one day, the small farm behind their house came up for sale. Mrs Belch owned it. Marcella wanted Pete to buy this farm for her and the family. Marcella went to her hidden jar, and gave the money to Pete. Because women had no rights until many years later, Marcella wanted Pete to take the money and buy that farm for them from Mrs Belch. Time wise, this would be about the time of the depression when money was sparse, but I believe it was some time before Dee was born. Marcella wanted that farm, because it was similar to the one where she lived when she was a child in Lithuania. Marcella wanted that farm, but Pete did not want any part of farming, and refused to buy that property. Marcella was extremely angry. Pete thought he had found a gold mine, when Marcella gave him the $2000. He took the money, went to his local tavern, and spent the entire sum on libations for his friends. He was known as a gambler at the tavern, and wanted to celebrate with his drinking friends. Pete had a reputation, he would bet someone that he could drink shots of whiskey, and beer all day long, and never get drunk. Even though he was a slight man, he never did get drunk, according to Dee, and always collected the betting money. He would stay all day Sunday at the tavern, instead of attending church services. Pete followed this routine, until all the money was gone. Pete had wasted all the money, Marcella had worked so hard to save. Much later, Pete knew he made a big mistake.

Now Pete did not want any part of the farm life, or land, and lost, and spent all the money Marcella had saved. And of course, from then on, Marcella despised Pete with a passion. She would cuss at him in the Lithuanian language all day long, about what a frog he was. I understand in Lithuania, the frog is the lowest form of anything alive. She never got her farm. Marcella stood on her back porch and yelled at Mrs Belch. But Mrs Belch had nothing to do with them not acquiring the farm. And from then on, Marcella would only wash Pete's clothes, when he came home on the weekends. She made him eat with a cracked plate, broken handled fork, and drink using a cracked cup. If Dee replaced his setting with good silverware and plate and cup, Marcella would then move his broken things back. Marcella did everything she could, to make Pete's life miserable, because of what he had done. Marcella wanted to kill him. A little later Marcella tried to hit him over the head with an iron skillet, because Pete had lost most of his eyesight, but John stopped her. It seems, there must not have been much love between Marcella and Peter, at any time. But they did have 6 children. Aside from their problems, Dee loved her grandmother and grandfather immensely. Dee never knew anything different, just love. Dee adored her grandmother Marcella. And the oldest son, John, Dee's father, was a king to Dee. After Pete retired, he realized he had made a huge mistake. He tried to make up for it by going to church on Sundays. He would sit through all the masses, Dee sat with him sometimes. Pete learned how to pray, and prayed a lot. I never knew if any of his children went with him, but Dee went to church every Sunday, plus attended the service daily, as a school child. She loved the school and the Nuns and the Nuns liked Dee a lot.

Sometime in the first years of Dee's life, while living with her grandmother, and grandfather, John purchased a hotel in Nicholson, Pennsylvania. It was about 10 miles from Scranton where his family lived. John must have been the manager of the grocery store, and managed the hotel too. John was always an adventurer. He hired his younger brother Sylvester and Sylvester's wife to take care of the hotel lounge/bar. But John did not know that Sylvester was an alcoholic. When John was not around, Sylvester would give away drinks to his friends. Dee said Sylvester's wife was a heavy drinker also. As a result, even though the hotel was very nice, John lost everything, money and all, because there were never any profits. This must have been around the time Dee's mother was in the hospital, but before her death.

At some point, John had purchased an old Jeep for transportation. It sounded to me that it must have been a used military Jeep. Dee said it was old. Anyway, John would take Dee out on Sunday afternoons, and drive around the countryside. Dee said they both loved that Jeep.

John would not divorce Dee's mother while she was alive, because of John's Catholic Faith. But after Mary (Dee's biological mother) died, John married again in 1946 to Dee's step-mother, her name was also Mary, and John and the stepmother were together for the rest of their lives. John was born in 1911, and died in 1991, according to Ancestry.com. I believe the step-mother was about 8 years younger than John. And I believe they both are buried in Virginia.

John was in WWII, Army. He was drafted at an older age and did not serve until late in the war. But WWII was still going on. He was married to Dee's mother then, as she was still alive. John ended his time in the Army and the war, with jungle rot on his feet. Dee never said the names of any countries where he may have served. His brother Sylvester was drafted, but accidentally shot himself in the foot during basic training, and never left the states. Sylvester collected disability for the rest of his life. John always complained about that.

After John's military service, and after Dee's biological mother had died, John married the step-mother. He had been managing a store, but was awarded a new job as an ambassador to Japan for the United States. This is around the time Dee was required to live with the step-mother, at about 7 years old. John's tour was for 2 years, but he may have been assigned a longer time. The step-mother was not a good housekeeper. And the step-mother used the money John sent her to run the household, to dress up and go out on Saturday nights, instead of spending it on cleaning supplies, and food. John had made an agreement with a good friend, and neighbor to rent this beautiful home to John, for the three of them to live. While John was gone, the stepmother never cleaned, rats came, ruined the place, and the owner made John move them out. Dee said the house had become filthy. The owner was a really good friend of John's, but became very angry about the ruination of his house. He had trusted John. Then John moved them into a condemned two story building, with no running water. The rats ran up the walls, across the floors, and would fight with each other frequently, which caused Dee to be very fearful of rodents. I never knew how long John and the stepmother lived in that place, but this is where Dee was living when at 2 or 3 in the morning she ran away to her Aunt Marion's house, which was within walking distance. Dee said John, who was now living back in Scranton, this must have been after the ambassadorship position, worked all the time, and was never home, even though it was terrible living conditions. Dee never said where the bathroom facilities were. I never knew if there were any babies living at this condemned place. And Dee said the step-mother never washed clothes. Aunt Marion had recently married, and had a nice clean home. Dee said her clothes came from thrift stores, second hand stores, and were mostly rags and Aunt Marion threw them away, probably afraid of lice. Dee told me she had lice in her hair, but it was never clear at what age, but I think it was when Dee lived with the step mother. Dee said the children at school would make fun of her clothes, and her red hair. Dee's life seemed pretty miserable after she was taken away from the grandmother's care. I wonder just how much John really loved and cared for his daughter. I wonder! Dee and Aunt Marion had lived in the old house with Dee's grandmother, years earlier, while Aunt Marion was still in school. Aunt Marion liked Dee, and Dee liked Aunt Marion. Dee said they shared a room. There was not much difference in their ages, maybe 6 or 8 years. This is probably why Dee decided to run to Aunt Marion's house when she ran away from the step mother.

Dee's Move to New Jersey

After Dee ran away to Aunt Marion's house, Aunt Marion told Dee that she could not stay there. Dee wanted to stay with Aunt Marion but John told Dee that she had to come back and live with the stepmother, or go to the orphanage or a foster home. Dee told them she wanted to go to an orphanage, or a foster home. Dee said she was not going back to live with the step- mother in their house! Dee was very firm about this. Then the family had a meeting of all members. It seemed no one wanted a 13 year old girl, but Dee's Aunt Pat in New Jersey, who already had 3 daughters, made a decision. Aunt Pat said Dee could live with her, but John had to pay support. Then Dee moved to New Jersey, to live with Aunt Pat. John did not pay any support then, and he never did pay any support. Because John did not pay any support, Dee was required to get a job, and pay her own way. Dee was fourteen years old by now. Dee found a job at the Prudential Insurance Company in New Jersey, running files from one department to another. There were tunnels under the streets connecting the offices. Dee worked at this job all through high school. Dee said the employees there liked her very much. Dee was allowed to keep half of her paycheck for purchasing her own clothes, and the other half went to Aunt Pat for board and care. Dee had to share one of the bedrooms with one of Pat's daughters. It sounded to me that Dee did not get close to Aunt Pat, nor her daughters, while she lived with them in New Jersey. I wonder how much love was in Aunt Pat's family.

Aunt Pat's husband was Uncle Frank. Uncle Frank was a butcher at the A&P (Atlantic and Pacific) grocery. Uncle Frank would bring home choice meats and groceries for the family. This family ate well. And Uncle Frank loved to smoke cigars. Plus Uncle Frank always wanted to watch the Friday night fights on TV. Aunt Pat allowed Uncle Frank to do this, but only on Friday nights.. So on Friday nights, Uncle Frank would be in his chair, cigar in hand, and a Stegmeir's beer beside him. Aunt Pat hated the cigar smoke, but she allowed him to smoke his cigars on Friday nights only.. And Dee did not like Aunt Pat's nagging Uncle Frank all the time, so Dee would sit with Uncle Frank, and watch the fights too. Dee said she liked doing this with Uncle Frank, he was a gentle man. Dee liked Uncle Frank. It seemed Aunt Pat was a habitual complainer and nagger. I do not think Dee liked Aunt Pat very much. It seemed to me that Aunt Pat never truly wanted Dee around.

While Dee lived with Aunt Pat, she only went back to Scranton a very few times. She probably was able to see her other Aunts, Uncle Sylvester, and her grandmother and grandfather too. But Dee never said anything about visiting her father, or step brothers, when she went to Scranton to visit family. And Dee never said that her father, at any time, came to visit Dee, or his sister, and family in New Jersey. The only time mentioned was at Dee's High School Graduation.

Some time later, Marcella moved to New Jersey, to live with Aunt Pat. I suppose after Aunt Pat's daughters had moved out of the house, and of course Dee had moved out. I could not find the year Dee moved out. Dee never told me of the ages of Aunt Pat's daughters, but there were three. I do not know if Dee was the older, or younger of them. It was 2017, when I learned Marcella had moved to Aunt Pat's home in New Jersey. Aunt Pat must have taken her mother in to care for her, because Marcella was getting older. I do not know the year Marcella moved, or how long she lived in New Jersey, with Aunt Pat. Marcella is buried somewhere in New Jersey, and Pete is buried in Nicholson, Pennsylvania. I did not get the date either of them died.

When Dee traveled to Scranton from New Jersey she rode the train. Dee likes the trains. Dee rode on the Pennsylvania Central Railway system. At that time, they were pulled by steam engines, as I remember. I remember the Penn Central railroads, especially the freight trains very well. The train tracks were at the back of the farm, where I lived. The water tank was also there, and the engines would stop to take on their water. We would wave at the train crew. Dee and I have gone to several train museums here in California and we have taken many short train rides.

While living in New Jersey with Aunt Pat, Dee attended Irvington High School. She had a few girlfriends, and they all used to go to the beach together. Dee ended up with some bad sun burns! Dee's fair skin, cannot handle the sun! When Dee graduated, the class had 350 students. Dee always had pretty good grades, and made the honor roll a few times. That was two of Aunt Pat's requirements, the honor roll, and paying her own way. At Dee's graduation, Dee never said if Aunt Pat attended, but John attended with the step-mother. Secretly, John gave Dee a wrist watch for graduation, but told Dee to never let the step-mother know where it came from. John was adamant about this. Dee said that was the only gift her father ever gave her.

After graduation, Dee worked as a waitress in Newark, New Jersey, and then some in New York City. She rode the bus all the time for transportation, and hated the humidity in the summer, and the cold in the winter. Dee did not like her clothes sticking to her back, because of the high humidity! Dee had waitress friends who wanted her to go to Florida to work, and said Dee could make lots of money from the rich people there. Dee said she did not like Florida, the humidity was high there too, and she did not want to go there, she wanted to go to California. For some reason, a little time later, John had some business in California. Dee went with her father to California the first time. But John did not stay in California, and went on his way. Dee must have gotten work right away, as she stayed in California for about a year. Then Dee wanted to go back to the east coast. She stayed only a short time back on the east coast, then decided she wanted to come back to California. Dee liked Hollywood. So there Dee was again, and she made many friends, mostly waitress friends, and acquired a nice apartment in Hollywood, Spanish style. Dee helped many friends over the years, and helped some get out of some serious trouble. I know Dee liked Hollywood.

One other story I remember was while Dee worked in New York City. Once as she was walking to work, there was a man standing on a soap box there on the street, and preaching the Gospel, or his message. Well it was Malcom 'X', so this must have been the late fifties, or early sixties. Anyway, he called Dee a "blue eyed devil" as she walked by. Dee did not respond, and paid him no attention. Dee has never been a racist. Dee is a very liberal thinker. We have since learned a lot about Malcom 'X'. He was very popular in the northern California area, in the 1960's. Some of his people remain here in northern California.

    I do not know much about Dee, and her travels between high school, and the time I met her. I know Dee was married before, maybe more than one time. Dee had it tough going from her childhood school, to the Aunt in New Jersey, and having to work to pay expenses her father had agreed to have paid. Dee probably connected to the first person who showed an interest in her. Dee did tell me that the marriage only lasted about 6 months. Dee's lips have always been sealed about her past, she must not have been very proud of some of the things that happened, or the decisions she made. We always agreed that the past was the past, whatever happened then was like water under the bridge, gone! Things like that are in the past, and do not matter now. We have always had that agreement, and honor it up to this day. So I think that when I came along, I made Dee happy, and Dee made me happy. I loved Dee at the very first moment of our relationship..

    Briefly back to Dee's family. For many years after we were married, I asked Dee, could we go back to Scranton, Pennsylvania, to see her childhood home and the school she attended, the area in general, and any members of her family still living there. Dee always said no, she did not want any part of going back, not even to visit. Dee must have had a lot of bad memories. I have always felt sorry for her, to not have some good memories of her childhood and past. Later on in this book, I have more information about Dee's childhood surroundings.

Our move to Oakland

One other important thing happened in August, 1971. After we had moved to Oakland in July of 1970, to a rented house on East 34th street, Dee saw this old reddish pickup truck in Alameda. It was at a gas station, and did not look too great! I had wanted a '55 Chevrolet pickup, but had not been looking seriously. This was a 1946 Chevrolet, 1/2 ton pick up truck. And it needed lots of work. But Dee liked it so very much, we bought it for $200. We then drove it to Oakland to the house we rented, put it in the garage, and I proceeded to work on it. I rebuilt the bed, painted the inside of the cab, flushed the engine, added another tail light, straightened the tailgate, and got the speedometer working. With fresh oil and a filter, the engine was running pretty good. It had the old 6 volt electrical system. I was told the engine had been rebuilt, and had about 30,000 miles on the rebuild, but after weeks of work, it was now driveable, and driving pretty well. The steering has always been very tough to handle. The transmission is the old 4 speed granny type, and you have to double clutch to shift gears. Over the years, I have done more work on it. I had it painted by Earl Schibb auto painting. I have since converted it to a 12 volt electrical system. I painted the frame, installed an all new brake system, and I was able to get the hand brake working properly. I worked on the steering, different tires, new spare tire and rim, and rebuilt the carburetor. I have made some other improvements over the years. Up till now, we have had it for 49 years. It has been used to help people move, hauled bunches of things to the dump, and other things a pickup truck does. Of course we hauled our supplies to the flea markets. Dee has always liked this old truck, and liked riding in it. I am thankful Dee liked it so much. It is almost a part of us. Sadly, Dee cannot ride in it anymore, as she cannot get up into it.

Over the years, we have made several trips to the flea markets, to buy things, and sell things too. I also made children's benches, and flower benches to sell, and we moved many of our excesses along at these markets. Dee loved the flea market. Problem was, Dee gave away our things too cheaply, and bought things at too high a price. If you had an honest face, you were sure to get a bargain from Dee. But whatever made Dee happy, made me happy, although at the time, I may not have felt too happy, and as forgiving as I should have been. We also went to the San Jose flea market in the truck, and it was big, the biggest flea market at that time. That trip was really fun, we both enjoyed riding in the truck. And the sales and bickering did not matter, as long as everyone was happy, that was the main thing. Dee was happy. That is what life is really about, happiness, and respect. If Dee was happy, I was happy. We would spend all day selling, and buying, and watching the people. Dee could have asked for just about anything, and I would try to please her. Over the years, she has asked me to drive people to their homes, or destinations. I never complained, and I did it because I loved this woman. I have always felt that Dee owned half of the car, and half of the truck, and she had the right to use them too. It was just that she could not drive either of them. Everything we have, we own together. We also loaned a few people money, they agreed to pay it back, but some never did. Dee has always been generous and forgiving!

When I met Dee, she had always worked as a waitress in the food service industry. She never wanted any part of being a cocktail waitress, Dee said that men wanted to pinch the waitresses' butts. Dee never liked to be touched, physically. I guess I was an exception, but I have been reprimanded several times. I have learned my limits. Dee worked as a waitress for 18 years, and was always a Union member. If she had worked 20 years, she would have gotten a pension from the Waitress and Bartenders Union. She thought about working as a waitress after retiring from Kaiser, but her physical health was not very good. She was always a good listener, very efficient, and always took time to listen to people and their concerns. And as you would guess, sometimes I would be asked for my help again. No problem. Some needed transportation to San Francisco or other locations. We loved going to San Francisco for anything. We made many hospital visits, helped in so many situations. Dee helped me move items to the dump, refinished items, many things over the years. Dee was always willing to try to help, any way she could.

Dee, the time I met her

When I met Dee, she was sharing an apartment with her friend, Mary. Mary had two daughters. The four of them had just moved to Ventura from Hollywood, and rented an apartment. Janet and her two children lived across the lawn in another apartment. This area of Ventura was more of an older area, but nice. Mary had a car and drove them to school, and to work. Mary and Dee both worked for the same restaurant owner. The owner had two restaurants. Mary worked at the older one, and Dee worked at the newer one, closer to my apartment. I do not remember what Mary's work hours were, but Dee worked the evening shift, and she would get off work at 9pm. They were both coffee shops, and did not serve any alcohol. I ate at Dee's restaurant several times. I also ate at the restaurant where Mary worked a couple times. Mary had had some personal problems when she lived in Hollywood. Mary was the reason Dee was in Ventura. Dee helped Mary and her girls move to Ventura, California, to get away quickly from those problems. Dee had to leave all her clothes and belongings behind, in the apartment in Hollywood. Mary and her children had to leave all their things behind too. Dee had a few dollars saved, to allow them to get the apartment in Ventura, California. Because of the urgency, Dee chose Ventura, California, to get out of Hollywood, quickly. Ventura is about 50 miles north of Hollywood, California.

Dee also had another wonderful friend back in Hollywood, Gayle, and Gayle had three daughters. Dee and Gayle had been best friends for quite some time, three or four years, possibly more. Dee used to babysit Gayle's daughters at times. Gayle was a very pretty woman. Beautiful skin, wonderful smile, beautiful laugh, coal black hair, dark brown eyes, soft voice, petite build, about 5' 2". Gayle was the kind of person that sticks in your memory, and who you never forget. A beautiful person all around, and fun to be around. Gayle and Dee had their birthdays in common, they were both born in the month of October, two days apart, but Dee was two years older. Gayle was a beautiful person, and her daughters turned out to be beautiful ladies too. After I had met Dee, and we were an item, I drove Dee to Hollywood to visit Gayle several times. We ate with Gayle a few times, watched the girls, visited the farmer's market, looked over Hollywood boulevard, and Dee showed me several sights while we were there. I do not remember very many of them, but Hollywood Boulevard and the Farmer's Market were a couple. It was fun. But we tried to spend as much time with Gayle as possible. The girls knew their way around to get to many of the sights. They all were such great hosts, how I wish we could do it all again!!

When Dee lived in Hollywood, Dee and Gayle worked at the same restaurant. There were two restaurants, one was a Jewish delicatessen. Mary also worked at one of them. I cannot remember exactly which restaurants Dee, Mary, or Gayle worked at. But they became very close over a short period of time. The restaurants were close to the movie studios in Hollywood, and close to the Farmers Market in Hollywood. We ate in the same restaurants where Dee had worked when we visited that area.

But a little later, Gayle moved on to working for a doctor. It was never clear exactly when Gayle made the change from the waitress to the office manager. Many things stick out in my mind about the things Dee told me about when she was working as a waitress in Hollywood. Before Dee and I met, while Dee was still living in Hollywood, she loved being a waitress. Dee has a remarkable memory. Dee knew exactly what people ordered, and would serve the food very professionally. Dee named some of the movie star people she saw, and some she waited on. She could even tell me about how some of the stars were dressed. Some waitresses tried to become friendly with some stars, but Dee only wanted to be a good waitress, and had no desire to have anything to do with the movie industry. I think Dee was so pretty, she could have easily caught the studio's eye.

Another story Dee told me about was while she was working as a waitress in Hollywood at the restaurant that was a Jewish Delicatessen. As I remember, the restaurant was close to the Farmer's Market. The Farmer's Market was a great place to shop for anything. And the market offered plenty of food to eat there, and take home, but it was more set up like fast food.. All kinds of things, and gadgets were for sale at the Farmer's Market. One day while Dee was at work in the restaurant, Red Skelton came in to eat. The chef at the restaurant saw Red come in. The chef must have liked Red, and asked Dee if she would ask Red for his autograph, to give to his son who was having a birthday. Dee got along with everyone, and joked around with the other workers, and would do almost anything asked of her within reason. Therefore Dee asked Red for his autograph, and explained who it was for. Red agreed and then asked Dee about the chef's children, how old was this child, and how many children did the chef have? Dee told Red that the chef had seven children. So Red took out seven pieces of paper, signed his name seven times, once on each piece of paper, and gave them to Dee. Dee then gave them to the chef. The chef was so happy! He sent out his thanks, via Dee. Everyone liked Red Skelton, and Red liked everyone. What a wonderful kind hearted story for all involved. And Red Skelton came in to eat at this restaurant many times after that. Red Skelton has always been one of our favorite comedians.

Dee told me about several other movie stars, and other Hollywood notables. One was Victor Borge, Dee said he was such a humble, likeable man. Such a great comedian too. She waited on Dan Blocker,(Dee did not like him), and some of the other Cartwright actors. There were several other stars Dee told me about, but my memory has forgotten. Dee showed me many of the sights around the area, especially the Stars on the sidewalk on Hollywood Boulevard. We visited Hollywood several times to visit Gayle, and her daughters, and they both showed me many places of interest, very many. Some big favorites were Disneyland, Universal Studios and Magic Mountain. Dee and I went to the Rose Parade in Pasadena, California one time.. But after a while, Dee said she liked Northern California better than Southern California. We always hoped Gayle would move here, to northern California. We had located a house up the street, which we were going to buy for her, and her daughters. But Gayle would not make the move, even though she liked being around Dee. That was too bad, as they all could have made a positive, new start. Gayle could have been successful at anything she wanted to do. We would gladly have helped all of them.

But I remember, once I drove Dee to Hollywood to meet some men who wanted Dee to be a "Go-Go" dancer in Las Vegas. Dee had beautiful red hair, a nice slim body, she weighed just 103 pounds, with blue eyes, a pretty lady, outside and inside. Dee was a star! They wanted her to forget me, and move to Las Vegas. I was not sure why we were going to Hollywood that day, but I would have driven to the end of the earth for Dee. So I guess she liked me more than being a dancer in Las Vegas. Dee told them she was never going to be a "Go-Go" dancer. We never talked about that subject again.

    We visited Gayle, and her family on our drive back to Indiana in 1968 and after we moved back to northern California, in 1969. Gayle and her daughters came here to visit us a few times over the next few years. Again, we offered to buy a house, if she would move up here. She turned us down. But we all visited. We also visited Gayle when she had come to San Francisco on business. Gayle and Dee were a team. They would restart their conversation where they had left off the visit before, maybe more than a year ago, it was amazing! Dee was very upset when she learned of Gayle's accidental passing, Dee lost her best friend in 1973. That was a bad year for all of us. My father died in February, my grandfather died the first of October, and Gayle died accidentally a few days later. A very sad year for all of us.

    After Dee and I were married, and moved to northern California, Mary and her daughters moved back to Hollywood, and we never saw any of them again. Mary and her daughters attended our marriage ceremony. I do not believe Mary was married, but she had two beautiful daughters who were very attached to Dee. We think of them often, and always hope they are doing well, and are happy. They were so sad, and cried as Dee and I left Ventura the evening after we were married. They wanted to stay and live with Dee. They were very attached to Dee. I asked Dee if she wanted to bring them with us, but Dee said they were Mary's children, and had to go with their mother. I listened to Dee and supported her, Dee knew best.

    Gayle and her girls were unable to be there for our marriage ceremony. Janet was there, and Connie (Janet's daughter) was Dee's bridesmaid. Connie P's son Michael was my best man and ring bearer. Connie P had brought the flowers for our wedding, I do not know who baked our wedding cake. It could have been Janet, or Mary, or maybe Dee. After the ceremony, we went back to Dee's apartment for the cake, ice cream, and sodas to celebrate. We also opened a few wedding gifts which had been given to us.

Many years have now passed. I previously had mentioned Gayle's accidental death at a young age. But Gayle's daughters have always stayed close in friendship. Sadly, one of Gayle's daughters has since died. We have remained close friends with Janet, and Connie P. When we talk on the phone, we discuss how their children are doing. Yes, they are all adults now, but we continue to wish them all well. The one surviving daughter of Gayle's has always remained close with Dee, by writing and visiting. The other children we have not seen for quite some time. We had visited with Janet, but many years ago. Janet is always super concerned about how Dee is doing when we talk on the phone. Janet says Dee is her best friend. I always want to stay in touch with Dee's friends, and of course, they are my friends now too. Janet and I talk on the phone frequently. Janet now lives in Texas. Connie P and I talk via the phone. Gayle's daughter calls, texts, and visits at times too.

Connie P, this lovely lady, worked with Dee in Ventura. She is a real sweetheart and is a good friend. We have stayed in touch since Dee and my marriage. Connie P still lives in the Ventura vicinity. Her son Michael lives close to his mother, and so do Connie P's grandchildren. She talks very highly of all of them. Connie P is such a good person. Her health has deteriorated some, mostly her vision. I always hurt inside when someone cannot see well. It comes to us older folks, but it's terrible. I had an uncle who was blind from Macular Degeneration. We have gone to see Connie P a few times. We always had good times visiting, seeing the sights, shopping, eating out, etc. Dee and I liked the drive there, about 7 hours. Connie P knows Dee is unable to walk, or talk now, but I put the speaker phone on, so Dee can hear the conversation. We talk ever so often, to stay in touch, and talk about how all of us are doing in life. I wish we could get together for another visit. I hope Connie P's vision gets better.

   Janet! Janet was a very good friend for Dee while they were all living in Ventura, California. Janet really helped Dee and Mary a tremendous amount. The four kids played together too. I had the honor of watching them a couple times. We all went to the dry river bed, and played with the rocks, and whatever else we found interesting. Janet has always remained a very close friend to Dee, even though Dee does not know anyone anymore. Janet sends cards, letters, and calls frequently. Janet moved back to Texas, not long after Dee and I were married. Janet was originally from Texas, and moved back to be closer to her family. Her two children remain close to her in Texas. Over the years, Janet has come to visit us a few times. We always have good times, and great subjects to talk about. Janet is just a good person. Dee did go to visit Janet in Texas, many years ago.. Dee said that while she was there they all played poker, and Dee kept winning. Dee liked to play card games, and she was lucky. Janet's health is not the greatest at this point in time, but she is always in my prayers. We do stay in touch by phone, I wish her and her family good health.

Dee, and her friends here, Fred

So many stories, some sad, but also many happy ones, and many with lots of laughter. A lot of elderly people with their own stories, many with no one to care for them. While Dee was working as a waitress, this story in particular stood out. I think this was about 1975. A 94 year old man, Fred, came to the restaurant every day for breakfast and lunch. Fred was always dressed in a pressed suit and tie, always looking very neat. Fred lived in a hotel nearby, on the second floor, about a block away. At the restaurant, they secretly named him Chop chop, because he would spend a large amount of time cutting up his food. This went on for quite some time, a couple years, and he was always proud of leaving a 25 cent tip. And of course Dee usually waited on Fred. The other waitress did not like Fred much, and made fun of him behind his back. Fred was not well off, monetarily. But one day, Fred did not show up to eat, nor the next day either. I know this is because I used to go to the restaurant after my work day at Del Monte, to pick up Dee at about 4pm. Fred had not shown up at the restaurant again, and Dee was concerned about Fred not showing up at the restaurant. I sort of knew Fred, because I had talked with him on a few occasions, so I went to his hotel and inquired about him. I was told at the hotel that he had to go to the county hospital, but they could not say what the problem was. Dee and I went to the hospital after work that day to check on him. We found him in such a bad condition! He had not been shaved, his face had not been washed, his eyes were almost matted shut, Fred looked terrible. Plus he had a breathing tube down his throat, and could not talk. Dee and I felt so sorry for him! It appeared the hospital was not taking care of him at all. They were just housing him until he died, and that is pretty much what they told me. Hospital care??? The next day, I shaved him, washed his face, cleaned his eyes, and talked to him. I did this for some time each day, because I visited him every day. They said he needed abdominal surgery. What is wrong, I asked? They said he had a bowel blockage, and needed surgery. I said, "Why can't you do the surgery?" Then I was asked if I was a member of his family, and of course I had to say no. If I was, they would have done the surgery. Fred told them and me he would sign the paper for the surgery himself. But they, the doctors, felt sure that the blockage was cancer. Fred had no living relatives in this area, only a niece living in the LA area. So I called her and told her of Fred's situation. I found out that she was not in much better health herself. The niece was in her 80's, and had limited walking. But anyway, she called and talked to

Fred's doctor. Fred had been in this hospital for about 10 days by now. She made arrangements to come up the following weekend, along with her granddaughter. The niece was not capable of traveling by herself. She came up the following weekend but Fred had died of the blockage rupturing before the niece could get there to sign any papers. What pain Fred must have suffered. After Fred died, the doctor wanted to do an autopsy, to find out the cause of his death. Thank goodness, the niece said no. And the niece told the doctor, "If you would not do the surgery before he died, you cannot do it now". I commend her for this decision. Fred's death was totally unnecessary. But before Fred died, Fred asked me to go to his room, if something happened to him, and get certain papers. After Fred died, I went to the hotel desk, and asked permission to go to his room, to his desk to get these papers, which Fred had told me about. The papers had all his funeral wishes written down. He had the grave sight purchased, the mortuary reserved, the song he wanted to be sung, which he had composed himself. Fred had it all written down, and all paid for. Because the niece was not going to be here right away, I called and asked her if she wanted me to handle the situation, and she said yes, to go ahead. Fred had it all there. All I had to do was follow his directions. Then I went to the mortuary, made their arrangements, found a lady to sing the song he had written for his own funeral, notified the cemetery, and purchased a few flowers. I paid $200 for opening and closing the grave, as those prices had increased over the amount Fred had previously paid. There was no money left for anyone. Dee and I grew to like Fred a lot. So sad to see him go like this. Of course, Dee and I attended his funeral, and went to the cemetery, to the grave site. I think there were 5 people at the service who were not the staff. The niece made arrangements at the hotel to dispose of Fred's belongings. And the niece thanked us for caring, and being so kind to Fred and thanked us for taking care of all Fred's funeral arrangements. She and her granddaughter were very kind people. It was an honor to care for Fred's last wishes.

Ralph

Then there was Ralph. His real name was Jack, but we all called him Ralph, I guess Dee gave him that name, as she did not know his real name. Ralph was never married. Ralph was a friendly guy, around 35 years old when we met him. His basic history, according to him, was that he was raised by his father. His father and mother divorced while the family was living in Seattle, Washington. Ralph must have been about 10 years of age, at the time of the divorce. Ralph had a sister named Pam. After the divorce, Ralph was raised by the father in Seattle, and Pam was raised by the mother. The mother and Pam moved to Texas. Pam later married, and had 3 sons. The mother and Ralph did not get along and became estranged, having no communication for many years. Pam and her mother were in some kind of ladies fashion business. After we met Ralph, he did go to visit his mother but said he would never do that again. We had urged him to visit his mother. We thought they might like each other after such a long time had passed. We hoped they could set aside bad feelings. It did not work! Ralph's father was a carnival worker, and taught Ralph all about the business, and how to con, swindle and trick people. Most carnival workers talk many people into spending money on chances. I think Ralph believed some of his own cons. Ralph was always a joker, and you did not know for sure when he was serious, or when he was joking.

Although Ralph had come into the restaurant where she was working, usually each day, Dee had not seen him for a few days. Ralph had his own legal business about a block away. Since she had not seen him for a couple days, when he did return, Dee waited on him and said, "You do not look so good. You look like your father just died." Dee meant it jokingly, simply because he was always playing and joking around about things. But this time he said, "Yes, you are right. I just came back from my father's funeral in Seattle." Of course Dee had meant it jokingly, but now she felt so sorry for the words she had just said. Dee had no idea that his father was even ill. Dee apologized profusely, but the words had been spoken. Ralph never held the words against her. And that was the beginning of the friendship between all of us. A difficult way of starting our relationship, but it was a wonderful friendship. Ralph even fixed dinner for Dee and me at his apartment in Alameda one time. He tried hard, used a blanket as a tablecloth, and cooked the food the way his secretary had told him to do. He had wine and all, and it was all very good. We gave him an "A" for everything. After that he never prepared any meals for any of us, but when we had something here at our house, he would bring something. And over time, Ralph came to our house many times for dinner. We all celebrated at our house, many birthdays, holidays, and probably many other reasons. We just liked getting together. Ralph was a good and friendly guy.

That evening Dee explained to me about what had happened at the restaurant, and the words she had spoken and asked,"What could be done, about the words said? How could Ralph deal with the memories of his father?" Ralph liked to drink alcohol, and sometimes a lot. He also smoked cigarettes. I was introduced to Ralph a few days later. The three of us started going out for meals, usually dinner houses. He would have a drink or two, but we did not. Ralph also liked the Oakland Raiders football team. Dee did not like football, so I attended a few games with Ralph. It was interesting. Ralph was really not a loner, although he did not have many friends that he mentioned, except an Indian friend named Milton. Dee and I did meet Milton one time. At Ralph's business, he had a secretary, Barbara. Barbara was married and had children. She was a very nice lady. Ralph gave her a tough time sometimes, and we expressed our opinions, because we thought he should treat her better. Then Ralph did start treating her better. But later, after several months, Barbara stopped working for Ralph. Then Ralph hired another lady, not helpful to Ralph at all, and then Ralph knew he had made a big mistake with Barbara. But Barbara refused to return to work for Ralph, after he had apologized and asked her to come back. Ralph also knew of another single lady, not the lady he hired to replace Barbara, who also worked for a similar business as his, which worked nearby. And it got to be that the four of us would go out for dinner, many times after we had met her. Later on, we found out that Ralph had proposed marriage to her, but she refused, as there was no love on her part. But they still remained friends. After a while, the owners of the restaurant where Dee worked were included in our going out to dinners and socializing. We all became friends. Then we would all go out, usually on a Saturday evening. However, the owners of the restaurant were alcoholics, and continually drank too much. We were unaware of that at first. But it all worked out OK. Dee and I learned how to handle them. After Dee had quit the restaurant work, the owners wanted to retire and sell the restaurant. They wanted Dee and I to buy it, and talked about a deal.. Dee and I talked about the offer, but we decided we did not want to be restaurant owners. We did not think it would be a good idea for Dee and me. We said no. They understood.

Sometime in 1977, Ralph purchased a house in San Leandro, California. He had purchased it before he had asked the lady for marriage, somehow thinking this might sway her answer. It did not. It was a very nice house, probably built in the 50's, a cute 2 bedroom house, 2 car garage, back yard, front yard, etc., and pretty easy to care for. And about this time, I had brought home this mother cat and four kittens, which I had found at work. The kittens were only a couple weeks old. We kept them all in our garage until the kittens grew bigger. We already had four kitties, that is why Dee was called the "Cat Lady". Ralph said he wanted two of the male kitties when they were old enough to wean. He then named them Harold and Milton. One cat was named after his Indian friend Milton, and the other after another person he knew named Harold. Much of his home furnishings in his house were of the Native Indian motif. Ralph also found this Indian statue, a seven foot tall Indian, made from wood. Ralph dearly loved this statue. Ralph called it his Indian Chief, or Chief for short. He was so proud of the Chief, it was the highlight of his life. Ralph did not cook, so there was no food in the house, only a couple boxes of cereal, but he did have a kitchen table and chairs. Ralph never disciplined the kitties we gave him. He had their kitty litter pans under the kitchen table, and there was kitty litter all over the kitchen floor. And the cats would get on top of everything. They slept anywhere they wanted. But this was a great friendship for all of us, cats and people. Ralph did not like all the shrubbery around his house, and had no lawn mower, or other equipment for caring for a property. Ralph did not really know how to take care of a house. So on weekends, Dee and I would take our truck, and equipment over, and mow, trim, and haul the remains to the dump. We gave him suggestions, how he could make his house more homey. Afterwards we would all go out for lunch or dinner, usually dinner.

The three of us went to Reno to gamble a couple times. Ralph liked to gamble, and he was lucky some, but lost too. He only wanted to go to casinos, where he could smoke and drink. It appeared to me, he would lose his money, because he bet large amounts. Dee and I always used our limits, and stuck with them. Then I would drive home.

Ralph was a good guy, but a little unusual. He loved Bob Dylan's music, and he adored WC Fields. Ralph loved his humor. In his home, Ralph had several records of Bob Dylan's, and a couple statues of WC Fields. No pictures, or much of anything else. Most walls were very plain. Not much furniture. No matter what we were doing, or where we were eating, Ralph would make comments like WC Fields used to do. Imitate him, sort of dragging out the words. We never judged Ralph, he had to do what he thought he needed to do. It was a good thing that he never married although Dee and I knew he was very unhappy and we thought he wanted a relationship like the one Dee and I had.

Around the first part of May of 1979, we had not heard from Ralph for a few days. Normally we would call each other about every day. I went by his house after work one day, I think it was a Monday, to see what he was doing. I rang the bell, knocked on the door, but he did not answer. I then looked through the window, and I could see him sitting in his chair. So I opened the screen door, the main door was already open, and went in, and said, "What are you doing?" He was just sitting there, like he was half dead. I said again, "What is going on?" He then told me that he had just come home from the San Leandro Hospital. He said he had been in the hospital for a couple days. The doctors had discovered that he had lung cancer. I felt so bad for him, and what he was telling me. I realized now, why, when I first walked in, he looked so terrible. It appeared to me that he was just waiting to die! Very depressed, and he was so very pale! Then I got him some water and a cookie or something like that. I think it was leftovers from my lunch box. I made him get up, washed his face, made him shave, fed his cats, and told him to get dressed. I cleaned the kitty litter while he was getting ready. Then we got in my car, and we picked up Dee. Dee was at home, after her workday. We told Dee about Ralph's condition. Then we all went out to eat. We took him back to his house that evening, after eating. We did not want to leave him alone, but he convinced us that he would be ok. But we did make arrangements to pick him up the next evening again, to eat out. He said he wanted to meet us at this restaurant the next evening. OK. But this time we had arranged for three other people to meet us at this restaurant the next evening. I told them the name of the restaurant. Ralph did not know about this arrangement. That was the last time Dee and I saw him that previous evening. He was to get together with us the next night. He did not show up at the restaurant. We called his house. There was no answer, and we went to his house, and found he had left a letter. Ralph had said that he was in Dallas, Texas with his sister. His sister was going to take care of him. He had flown out during the day, while we were at work. Ralph just left the house, kitties, and everything. He had given us a key sometime earlier. We called his sister, and asked what was happening. Ralph would not talk to us, but his sister did. In his letter he had said that he did not want anything, and to see if someone would take the cats. He made arrangements with the neighbor, they were going to buy his house. He had arrangements for the car dealer to pick up his car. Ralph had not taken anything with him. He said in his letter to do anything we wanted to with all his possessions. A friend did take the cats, and another friend found a business to purchase the home furnishings. But his new clothes, the Indian Chief statue, so much of what he loved, was left behind. Dee and I, after thinking about Ralph, agreed I would take one of my wooden boxes over, and put all his good clothes in it, along with a couple of small statues of WC Fields. He had left behind many very nice clothes. He had Pendleton shirts, cowboy boots, and other good clothes, etc. I put the best in the box. Then I rolled the Indian Chief, as he called him, in a carpet, and tied it tightly. All the rest of his clothing we took to the Salvation Army store. I brought the wooden box back to our house, and the Indian Chief rolled in the carpet. Then I had a moving company come by and pick it up, and we sent it all to Dallas, Texas, to his sister's house. Ralph's sister knew it was coming, but

Ralph did not, until it arrived. Dee and I paid for the shipping. Ralph was so very happy! Ralph then talked to me over the phone, thanked me, and said that I sent all the things he really loved. Of course he was so very happy to get that Indian Chief. And even though he said he did not want anything, we sold what we could, and was able to send him a check for $1,200. When we last left his house, it was very clean. We later learned that Ralph died from lung cancer in September of 1979. Ralph had only been in Texas for about 3 months. We were able to keep in touch with his sister for a few years, but she had health problems too, and we have now lost contact with her. I think of Ralph often, drive by his house once in a while, and miss our good friend. Dee and I only knew him for about four years.

Ralph's sister Pam, was a very pretty, petite woman, but she had terrible back problems. She did tell us, before we lost contact, that she had several surgeries on her back, but was always in terrible pain. We talked to her over the phone, exchanged Christmas cards, learned a few things about her three sons, which she adored. But that was the last we heard from her. Pam and her husband, and three sons came to visit Ralph, here in San Leandro, California, the year before Ralph became sick. Her sons were around the ages of 8 to 10 years of age then. An adorable family. I believe Pam was a year or two younger than Ralph. We never did meet Ralph's mother. We know she attended Ralph's funeral. Ralph is buried in Texas. Ralph enjoyed his nephews. He used to fly into Las Vegas, Nevada and his sister would send one of her son's to Las Vegas too. Then the two of them would join one of the guided trips down the Colorado River. Ralph enjoyed that so much, he talked about that extensively. I do hope Pam's sons enjoyed it too. He said it was about a week long trip, and lots, and lots of fun. They camped, swam in the River, had chores to help the crew with, and the crew fixed the meals. They must have had a really good time! Sounds like fun to us! Ralph had done this for a couple years, maybe more, with Pam's sons.

There used to be a little restaurant on East 12th street, in East Oakland. It was called the Fruitvale Crab Pot. It was owned by a man named Roland. Roland's wife, who was of French ancestry, was the chef/cook at this restaurant. Ralph had become very good friends with Roland, probably because Ralph never cooked, and always ate his meals out. Ralph raved so much about the wonderful food served at this place. Roland's wife was a wonderful chef, and it was French cuisine of course.. She made everything taste delicious. Dee and I never went to this specific restaurant, because the building, the one the restaurant was in, was sold and the restaurant had to be moved. I believe the original building has since been torn down. But Roland moved this restaurant to Crockett, California. It was located under the Carquinez Bridge, with a beautiful view of the bay and bridge. It sat between the Amtrak/freight train railroad tracks, and the bay waters. I am not sure of the restaurant's name, but I think it was called The Nantucket Fish Company, again I am not sure. Anyway, Ralph took us there many times. I usually drove, as Ralph drank some. But when we walked in and Roland, the maitre d', saw Ralph, he would seat us at one of the back tables. This restaurant probably held 50 to 60 customers. He pretty much brought us his favorite food, as I do not think we ever ordered from any menu. Roland treated us like royalty. Roland brought us samples of everything. But my favorite was this crab dish, baked in a little crock style dish, with cheese on top. It took some time to bake, about 30 minutes after you ordered it. Probably had many calories, but golly, was it good! I do not remember exactly which dish Dee ordered, as Dee was not fond of crab meat. But whatever it was, Dee enjoyed it. Of course, Roland was sort of a flirt, but Dee was never impressed by any man attempting to get her attention. But we three would sit and eat, Roland would sit with us for a moment or two, and talk with us when he was not seating customers. It did not matter what time we arrived at the restaurant, we could not leave. Roland would stop us, and tell us, "You cannot leave". Then Roland would bring a bottle of his Cherry Vishnick liquor, sit it on the table, and he would tell you, "You cannot leave until this bottle is empty". This liquor was an after dinner aperitif, from European manufacture. Sometimes Roland would sit and have a sip. As the night of business for the restaurant slowed down, Roland would bring his wife out of the kitchen, and introduce her. We all sat around the table and talked about the food, business, and the many many compliments. A very pretty lady, and a wonderful chef!! We commented about the atmosphere, it was mostly the wife's design. Very relaxing, and enjoyable. We usually left the restaurant around 11pm, even if we had arrived there at 7pm. As we were leaving, we customers had to watch for the trains coming, when walking across the train tracks, as the trains, both freight, and Amtrak, ran along there frequently. You could feel the vibrations inside the restaurant as the trains passed by. The parking lot for trucks and autos was on the other side of the train tracks. The restaurant sat on the edge of the bay water, and there was a commercial fishing business next door. We enjoyed dining there so much, we would still be going there if we could.

    Ralph had another good friend, named Romano. Romano owned his own pizza restaurant in Alameda, Ca.. Romano had come to this country from Italy, and opened this business. My goodness, he could make the most delicious pizzas and other pastries. His cakes were top of the line, exceptional!! Yes, he was busy, especially on the weekends. Over time, we ordered many pizzas and cakes for different occasions. Behind this restaurant was a house which Romano owned, and Romano used it to store all his supplies. No one lived in it. He used tons of flour, and other ingredients, cake icings, oils, etc. and stored them all in this house. He also used this house for meetings with his employees. The house was livable, had a bathroom, bedrooms, and a large living room that had this large table in the middle, with a few chairs and all the supplies stacked around the walls. Lots of ingredients, all kinds for baking, were stacked there. Romano used this room for all kinds of meetings but he let a few special friends use it too. Ralph talked to Romano, and arranged for Betty, the owner of the restaurant where Dee worked, to celebrate her birthday there. It was a surprise birthday for her. Ralph told Betty the celebration was going to be at his house, meaning Romano's room behind the restaurant. Of course this was not really Ralph's house. Betty was pretty gullible, and she liked to drink bourbon. Of course, Romano knew we were going to order pizza, and a big cake from him. Romano was aware of the surprise we had planned. When the evening came, we arrived early to set up decorations, and then Betty arrived. She just could not understand how Ralph could live in a house like this! And of course, Ralph kept egging her on! Dee had a big part in pulling this off, as a surprise, and helped with this entire evening. Dee and Ralph had made all these arrangements, they both were very good at surprise parties like this. The evening was a huge success. Betty just could not believe Ralph could live in such a house. We laughed and laughed until we cried. Romano's pizza was super, and the cake he made was exceptional. Dee and Ralph told Betty the next day that that was really not Ralph's house, and gave her the whole story. This was an evening none of us will ever forget, and we reminisced for a long time afterwards. Reminiscing always made us cry from laughter. Dee and Ralph could really cook up some great ideas. We lost a great friend, when Ralph died.

    At the last restaurant Dee worked, and after Dee had retired from waitress work, the owner sold the restaurant and retired. The owner had been putting off some surgery for some time and decided to have it done after his retirement. The hospital did the surgery. But something happened inside his body after the surgery, and he died from the problem. It was so sad to watch a person die this way, even though he only suffered a couple days. We had become pretty good friends. His wife died of a broken heart about three years later. The wife's birthday was the same day as my mother's, but my mother was one year younger. The wife had originally come here from Canada, but never said anything about her family there. Sad lives, to end that way. They did have a daughter, we do not know what happened to her. Sometimes, I visit their grave sites, here in Oakland.

Walter

Then there was Walter, another friend Dee met at the restaurant. Walter must have been around 62 years old at that time. He was another sad soul who needed help. Walter worked at the PG&E utility company's office building a few blocks from the restaurant here in downtown Oakland. He must have been part of the mail room, as his job and responsibilities were in the basement. He gave us a tour one time, but I cannot remember all the details. His job was created especially for him, by his family, to keep him out of trouble. He did not have much to do there, but he liked it. He worked there for many years. His parents and relatives were big wheels at the company in the beginning, when the company was expanding. They lived in San Francisco, but some of the family moved to Oakland after the 1906 earthquake. Walter was never married. Walter was very smart, but he never said anything about attending any college. He was well-educated. He always wore a suit, white shirt, and necktie. Always! He was tall and skinny, and never gained weight. He always looked neat, and clean, suit pressed. But he would say some of the craziest things, at any time. You never knew when to take him seriously. He was a lot like Ralph in that category, but Walter had a bad case of nervousness. When he was in the Army in WWII he was assigned to military tanks as a radioman. He had shell shock. All of his mannerisms were as a result of the war experiences. His mind was good, he was smart, just a character! He looked a lot like a tall Hitler, full mustache and all., stood straight, very nice appearance. His parents were from Germany. His favorite thing to say was, "Bomb Them", if he did not like something someone was saying. People learned that he was crazy. But he really was not. It was just the personality he had developed. We liked Walter, but we knew to keep him at a distance.

Walter came into the restaurant where Dee was working each day to eat lunch. I did not think he came in for breakfast, but I later found out that he did. And he often complained to the owner about the food, not the taste or quality, just that the portions were not big enough. Walter could eat a lot. And he was right, the portions were kind of small. The owner was a good cook, just stingy about portions. Walter asked the restaurant owner to put more food on his plate. I do not think the restaurant owner did, although he may have that specific day, but I recall him serving skimpy portions most of the time. I ate there a couple times myself. But the owner's wife was a terrific cook.

After some time, Walter had been missing from the restaurant. Somehow, Dee learned that Walter had been mugged, beaten up, and was in a rehabilitation center close by. We visited him there. And Walter had recuperated, after a short time. At that time he was living in a very cute apartment in East Oakland, not far from where we live. It was a predominantly Africanamerican community. Walter, being Caucasian, probably made a statement that someone did not like, as he was known for that. This is probably why he was beaten up. He was told by the authorities that he needed to move from there. The hospital had assigned him a social worker. Dee and I volunteered to move him. The social worker acquired an assisted living space for Walter to move to, but had no space for anything else. When we arrived at his apartment with our truck to move him, I had brought some boxes. Walter had model airplanes everywhere. In cabinets, everywhere! Must have been an easy 100. Plus he had a model tank collection, a small train set, and a few clothes, one suit, and a couple of shirts. He had a barometer that belonged to his parents when they lived in San Francisco, which had fallen during the 1906 earthquake, and it had a small chip on it. He also had a beautiful oak desk, although he had ruined the top surface. Walter had several hand tools, all of good quality for making these models. So we boxed all the airplanes as best we could, without breaking them, and put them in our truck. This was a handful. We had to make 2 trips. Then we moved all these model airplanes and the tanks into our garage and some things into our house, with the understanding that he would find a more permanent home for all these things. After about a year, there was very little space left to work in our garage, and I insisted we had to move all Walter's things. I told Walter he needed to find a place to take them. Walter finally did find a hobby shop that would take the airplanes. I forgot, he also had model ships too. Beautiful ships, but requiring space we did not have. But it ended up, we moved the airplanes to a hobby shop in San Leandro. I had the desk refinished, and put it in our house. I stored the ships in our crawl space above the kitchen. That worked until the roofers dropped a board on them and ruined the clipper ships, and all the others. Walter had wanted to live in our back bedroom, in our house, but Dee and I said no to that. Walter lived in the assisted living home, but made several trips to hobby shops in San Francisco. And guess what, he was making more models of tanks, and other little things while living there. We visited him several times at the assisted living place. He lived there a few years, because it was so close to bus lines, as Walter never drove a car. When Walter died, it must have been quick, as we never knew what happened. to him, or his things. We never knew what date he passed. The assisted living facility would not give us any information, because we were not family. The fact the family was German makes me think the family was sort of secretive. Walter was a good guy, but different. One time we took him to the Watsonville Airplane show, where there were all kinds of old airplanes. He loved being there, seeing the planes flying in the air. We could look at all of them while they were on the ground. He especially loved the old WWII airplanes. But guess what: Dee told him he could not wear his suit to an airplane show and, besides, it is pretty hot where the show was taking place. Dee had purchased a new blue shirt, new pants, and I do not know what else for Walter, and he wore them that day, but we never did see him in those clothes again. We do not know what he did with them. But we did spend the whole day there at the air show, we all enjoyed seeing so many planes, and other exhibits. Yes, I had to buy all our food, as Walter was a little stingy with his money. But we all had a good time.

Harry

We had a wonderful Chinese man and woman who were our neighbors, when we lived at the rented house. The man was born in Canton, China, and immigrated to the US, as a young man. He was married to a lady, an arranged marriage by her father, but she was a little strange. They had no children, as Harry was about 30 years her senior. He was a very happy man, but she was not a happy woman. He was always giving us flowers, and when the wife baked Chinese cookies, Harry would bring some to our house. After we moved here to Rosedale Ave, he came to visit many times, and we went to visit them at their house a few times. But the lady was not friendly to Dee. Dee was pretty, with red hair, and I think the lady was jealous. I felt this lady was a threat to Dee, I could not trust the lady. But this Chinese man was a very nice person, a kind and loving person. He loved Chinatown, both in Oakland, and also San Francisco. He was always showing us the Miss Chinatown young ladies pictures, in competition for their calendars. They were all pretty. He would ask me to judge, and tell him the one I liked the best. Then he would tell me the one he liked best. And after Miss Chinatown was crowned, he would tell me which lady won the competition. As for the lady who won the competition, I have no idea if she was the one he picked, or the one I picked. He and I also came up with an agreement. This was his proposal: I would drive him and his wife to dinner in my car, and he would buy dinner for Dee and me. I talked with Dee and we agreed to do this. We all went to downtown Oakland Chinese restaurants and I drove us to Chinatown in San Francisco, to the Chinese restaurants. All were dinner houses, with very good food. Not every dinner, but most of the dinners were for someone's birthday, graduation, or other celebration for someone he knew. He always said one or more people were his cousin, or cousins. I wondered about that. We were never to bring any gift, he said he would take care of all gifts. He always introduced Dee and me as his good friends he would say. Dee and I never complained, and we were usually the only Caucasian people at the celebration, with many times over a hundred in attendance. I had no idea what exactly we were eating. If Dee did not like hers, she would move it over for me to eat. Dee and I did not speak or know the Chinese language. We enjoyed being there, and supporting our friend. He was quite elderly.

    This Chinese man and I worked on several projects. One was installing a new hood over their range in their kitchen. I had to make a cabinet to hold the vent. We also put a French drain all around their house. When we moved here to Rosedale, he gave us so many potted plants, all of Chinese origins. He wanted us to have them, it was OK. Sadly, Harry died at some point, but we never knew when. I knew the man had been sick, we visited him while sick, but his wife never told us of his passing. She did not even want us to visit him. She would not tell us when he died, or where he is buried, or what he died from. I am not sure of his age. I do not think his birthday was ever recorded properly in China. But he told me when his birthday was, and that he was 90+ years old. I lost a good friend when he died, I liked Harry. Harry was his name, yes we lost a good friend..

Rosedale Neighbors, Phil

Phil lived next door to us, when we moved here to Rosedale Ave.. Phil was another character. But not one that Dee acquired as a friend, because Phil came with our new neighborhood. He lived next door, owned the two houses next to him and rented them out. He was very concerned about who lived next to him. But I guess he came to like us. He was a little odd. He moved here originally with his mother, but she died before we moved here. I do not know how long Phil and his mother lived next door before she died. Phil's nephew, and his family lived next to him. Phil never married. He never owned a car; he walked everywhere. He worked all his life for Stokely Van Camp, on East 14th street. Phil lived close enough to this company factory for him to walk to and from work. He would not ride the bus. If Phil had an appointment downtown, he would walk. He always worked the evening shift, and would get very angry if I made noise during the day when he was trying to sleep. Of course, I did not know this at first, but I learned this when he told me. Phil was very smart. I don't know if he had any college education, but he read all kinds of books. Phil must have had 500 or more books in his house when he passed. He had so many books, the weight broke the flooring joists in the house, in a couple places. Some books were very valuable, most all were hard backed.. Phil gave us a couple, which we still have. Phil told me he had three stamp collections, plus extras. He showed them to us a couple times, and would explain the stamps, their cost, their country, etc. He knew all about stamp collecting. Many stamps were very rare, and cost a lot for collectors. At that time, just prior to his death, he told me the one collection was worth $150,000, and that was in 1980. The other collections were not as complete, but had to be worth quite a sum of money. Phil had an "A" type personality. Because he was always in a hurry to do things, talked fast, etc.. He seemed like a nervous type of person. It appeared to me that Phil did not spend much time preparing himself for whatever he wanted to do. Just impatient. And as I said before, Phil would never sit down when he came into our house! Phil must have had some hand tools at some point, but none that I saw. The reason I say this is because on one hand he had only one finger and a thumb and on the other hand, he had only two fingers with nub's where the missing fingers had been.. Both hands had fingers when he was born. But he told me that he ran his hands through a table saw, and was not careful enough, and therefore cut off the fingers plus part of one thumb. I am sure that is what happened. No one would do that intentionally. I cannot imagine the pain! I worked with him on a couple projects, Phil was very impatient!

    I do not know if Phil had a working clothes washer, I know he had a washer, because I saw it. But he never wore clean clothes. We bought him a sweater for Christmas one year, and he wore that sweater for months. He never washed it, and it had food stains all down the front. Phil was a pitiful soul. When he came into our house, he would never sit down. He would not come to our house for a sit down dinner. We invited Phil several times. To help him, Dee would prepare our dinner, make a plate for Phil, and I would take it over to him. Probably the only decent meals he had after his mother died. He said his mother died a couple years before we moved here. Phil and his nephew would talk/mostly argue about things sometimes, and both of them could cuss up a streak, believe me! Phil's nephew and family lived next door to Phil. That family could really argue, and yell! I do not think they liked me at all. The nephew had a wife and two daughters. I tried to help Phil when I could. I mowed his lawn, helped him put in a new water line, etc. nothing big. I was in his house many times, he never cleaned anything. His chair had all the coverings worn off, just bare wood exposed, but it was an overstuffed chair at some time. Phil liked Dee a lot, and appreciated her cooking, and our caring about him. Phil had a Labrador dog named Cindy. She died a year or two before Phil. I think Phil died about 1980, not sure of the date. He was a reader, and collector of all these books. After Phil died, the nephew and niece inherited Phil's house. They brought a dumpster in, parked it in the driveway, and threw all Phil's books in it. They all went to the dump. Some of those books were collector items, and libraries would have loved to have several of those books. Many were quite valuable. Tons of information! And after Phil died, the nephew and his wife came into our house, looking for things Phil might have given us. We only had two books, but they did not see them. They were jealous, and wanted anything Phil may have had that was of any value. Phil was a character, but not mean like the nephew. Dee and I liked Phil, and to some extent, we felt sorry for him. This is why we tried to help him, and give him some decent food to eat.

Neighborhood Children

When we moved into this house in 1971, there were several kids who lived on this block. Chris was the most popular, and pretty much the leader. He must have been about 9 or 10, at the time. And there was Earl, Robert, Laney, Monte, Camaya, Tina, Torrie, Roy, Terry, Gordon, Olivia, Tasha, Billie, John, Corky and the Chan children, probably more.

There were some who came from around the corner. On Saturdays, most of them gathered around our house, because it was always open, and Dee usually had some cookies that she had baked earlier in the day. Dee was so helpful to all of them. She was a great hostess. Dee was, and is, just a beautiful person. Many of those kids periodically stop by our house, to say Hi, even though it has been so many years. They all want to see Dee. They remember Dee, even though it has been almost 50 years. They never forgot Dee, and her kindness, Dee had the younger ones in the house, reading to them, or playing little games, coloring books, etc.. Dee treated them like their 2nd mother. Dee loved it, and loved all children. Some of us, and the older ones, would be throwing the ball around to each other in the driveway, or the front lawns. We also played table tennis in our garage. Some were helpful too. They helped me mow the lawn, clean up, trim bushes, etc..That was when we had lawns to mow. They would help me clean the garage, wash the car, and wash the truck. Sometimes I would ride them around the block in the truck, with them in the back end. Yes, that would be illegal now. But I never went fast, and they pretty much followed my rulings. I never had any problems with the kids. Dee and I always enjoyed all the kids being around. and there were some neighborhood dogs too. The dogs were fun, Ringo being one. She was lovable, and great to have around. They never chased the cats, everybody got along, even the cats and dogs. We hid the dogs from the Animal Control people, because they were supposed to be on leashes but were not. No fighting was allowed by anyone. They all had to go home if something like that started, and after the first time, we did not have that problem again. Probably the reason for so many kids around may be because the elementary schools are about a block away. The high school is a couple blocks, the Catholic school is not far, easy walking distance. It has always been a mixed nationality neighborhood. We enjoyed all of those kids.. We remained in contact with some. Most of them went to college, married and had families of their own. Chris married, and has 5 kids of her own, and lives on the East Coast. Some stop to visit once in a while. Dee was always the first one to make friends with the kids in our neighborhood. When we lived in the apartment in Alameda, Dee knew all the kids. When we moved to the house which we rented in Oakland before we moved here, Dee had some of the neighbor kids coming in. When we moved here, Dee made friends with the neighborhood kids, and acquired more friends. Dee is just a loving, kind person, and always has been. That is why they, and I, always loved Dee. Dee is a remarkable person!

Rosedale Neighbors

When we moved here on Rosedale Ave, we acquired several wonderful neighbors, and still have many today. Some are now deceased. Dee usually rode the bus to work at first, as it is a two block walk, and the bus runs frequently. Dee worked at a restaurant downtown. Ruby also worked at the same restaurant as a dishwasher. Ruby lived close by, and would meet Dee at the bus stop. Ruby's husband worked at a lumber company not far away, and gave me lots of scrap wood leftovers. Ruby and Dee rode the bus together to get to work. Many neighbors also rode the bus, they did not need cars. Many people in this neighborhood did not own automobiles in the early 70's. Virginia and Eddie also lived close by. They were husband and wife, both from Pennsylvania originally. Both were deaf. Eddie had poor eyesight. Eddie worked at a foundry somewhere in Berkeley. The three of us, Eddie, Dee and myself, would walk to the bus stop, meet Ruby, and I would wait until they were all on the bus. Then I would walk back home. I did not need to be at work for another hour or more.

There was another really nice man who lived around the corner who walked with us sometimes. I do not recall his name. I believe Dee and Ruby sometimes rode the bus home together too. But we became good friends with Virginia and Eddie, and their sons. We did our best to communicate with them, I never could pick up sign language. Over the years, we visited them. Dee baked things and gave them to them. Virginia cleaned our house for a while. I helped Eddie do a couple projects around their house. They went to Pennsylvania to visit their relatives on occasion, and their relatives visited here too. We would be invited to their get-togethers. Their get-togethers were somewhat unusual. No talking, but all sign language. Really interesting for me and Dee. Dee and I were very happy to see all of them having such good times. Virginia and Eddie were very excited when their son John took them to Hawaii. They talked about Hawaii for a longtime after the trip. They were just great people. Sadly, Virginia and Eddie have since passed. Their sons are very successful young men. Dee was responsible for their friendship, and many other friendships.

Other neighbors to mention are Charles and Joanie. They moved into the house across the street about a year after we moved here. They were young, and had two children after they moved here, Monty, and Comaya. Charles worked as a machinist. Joanie was a nurse at Kaiser Hospital here in Oakland. Their son became a doctor. Charles and Joanie divorced after a few years, and Charles remained in the house. Charles was also a little different, because when he came into our house to visit, he would never sit down. I never knew why he could not sit down. But he would talk for an hour, and never get tired of standing. Charles also had some wonderful, large model airplanes in their basement. On Saturday mornings, he would put one of them on the street surface, start their engine, and run them up and down the street. He would fly them at the local model airfield too. The planes were exciting to learn about them, and about flying. Several people fly model airplanes. I never knew so many people liked that hobby! Somehow, I think the house was foreclosed on Charles. He came to visit a couple times after he had to move, but we also heard later that he passed.

Pat and Lionel moved in next door, in 1974. They were parents to two daughters. Dee and I later became the daughter's God Parents. Pat and her daughter still live there. Lionel died several years ago. We have not seen the younger daughter for a long time.

Mrs. Taylor lived up the street, and came to visit frequently on Saturdays. She had a cute little Chihuahua dog. The dog was very overweight. But it walked in our house, never paying any attention to our kitty. Mrs Taylor was a very nice lady. She later moved to northern California to live with her son. We liked her visit, it was very interesting to talk with her.

Marva was a great lady who lived a couple houses away. She had a wonderful husband named Zack. They had several children, who grew up in this neighborhood. Zack owned and operated an automobile body repair shop, here in Oakland. Sadly, Zack died a young man. And sadly later in Marva's life, she accidentally caught her sweater on fire, while cooking on her kitchen stove. She died from her injuries shortly afterwards. Marva used to visit frequently. She would come and sit in our kitchen. Marva liked to talk with Dee. Marva was a beautiful person and interesting to talk with. Marva also owned the neighborhood dog, Ringo, a great dog. We have lost many good neighbors! There are several more neighbors whom I could mention. Many moved to other neighborhoods, retired, children grew up, etc..

We have always had a good neighborhood. Some people are more friendly than others, but that goes everywhere. Yes, many houses have sold, and resold, but the newer people are always looking out, to maintain as high a standard of neighborhood as possible, and the neighborhood continues to improve. There are committees that are trying to upgrade the landscape. And there are neighborhood watch groups. Most neighbors are looking out for one another. There are websites now that people keep up with, telling of things for sale in the neighborhood. It also tells about the crime in this area. As I had said before, in the 49 years that we have lived here, we have seen many children grow up, travel on, get educated, and develop a lively hood to fit themselves and their families. Most of them we do not have contact with now, but we do think of them at times, and hope all are well, happy, and leading a good and successful life. At one time, there was a homeowner close by, who was in the illegal drug selling business, and partying. That lasted about 6 months, and with the neighbor's complaints and the police coming, that ended and they moved. Good riddance!! Many people have always put Oakland down because of the crime level. There is crime everywhere, not only in Oakland, but Oakland has its share. Oakland is sort of a sleepy place, and has always been the bedroom community of San Francisco. Oakland basically became a city after the 1906 Earthquake in San Francisco. People there decided to move to Oakland, and build new homes after the earthquake. It seems to me, it is the attitudes of people that make a neighborhood good or not good. I always pray for a safe and friendly neighborhood, which we now have.

There have always been children living near us. There was a Spanish family who lived next door to us. They moved away in 2009 I believe. Part of the family moved to Arizona, and part of them stayed around here in the Bay area. There were five boys in the family. We enjoyed visiting with the boys. Dee and I took them to several fun events for all of us. We went go-kart racing, competed in different games, and other things kids want to do. They liked to eat out, but they especially liked ice cream. So we usually stopped for ice cream, after eating something. A couple of them have married and had children. We were told of another getting married at a later time. We have pretty much lost all contact with them. They have all gone their own way and we do not know how they have made out. They had lived in that house for approximately 20 years. We saw the littlest one grow up. He was the only one born here, while the family lived here on Rosedale. The youngest caused his mother and father lots of strife as a baby, because he had so much energy. The parents were out almost every night, walking him up and down the sidewalk, to wear his energy down some. The boys would all be in their 40's now. The parents moved to Arizona, and the last we heard, they were having some medical problems. We hope they are doing well. They were all good people.

    A great young lady, who has lived up the street for many years, purchased the house next door after the Spanish family moved. I remember this little girl from the time she was about three years old. She and her brother used to come down to our house to play with the other kids on the weekends. She was very small, and all the other neighborhood kids were much older. Dee entertained the younger ones, and the girls that were not tomboys. As time moved along, this young lady purchased the house, moved in, married, and now has a son. She is such a good person too. We always wish everyone peace and happiness. Her father has come to visit us many times. He and I talk about things happening all around, and love to criticise politics. His wife (the daughter's mother) has MS, and he cares for her, along with their son. This young lady, and her family have lived next door for about 10 years and her parents have lived up the street for about 40 years. Happily, this young lady is expecting another baby!

Dee's Shopping

Dee loved to shop. Many years ago, there were two big department stores in downtown Oakland. Dee could go to these stores and look and shop for hours and hours! We would agree to meet at the restaurant in the basement at a certain time after we both got off work. It always worked out well. I never had to worry about birthdays, or holidays, as Dee would always buy cards, gifts, for whatever the occasion was. Dee loved to do this. Dee never spent much money, she knew how to manage. And if there was anything heavy or large, we would purchase that, after we met that evening. Several items in our home now were purchased at these stores many years ago. Dee worked in a restaurant, but she loved to eat out too. That is why we would meet at restaurants. Capwell's and Rhodes Department stores were in downtown Oakland. Capwells had a wonderful cafeteria in the basement, plus they had all their bargain priced things in the basement too. It was a great place to meet, and Dee could easily wait for me. As we were eating out over the years, we always talked about things that were important to us. And we would make our decisions together. I am sure this is the reason that we never argued about things. We talked things out and made our decisions and stuck with them. Some small and some big. Downtown Oakland had other wonderful food places to eat, several cafeterias, along with many mom and pop restaurants. There were not any chain restaurants at that time in downtown Oakland. Oakland used to be a very popular, and busy city. Many people have since moved to the suburbs. Now, there are not any cafeteria style restaurants downtown, such as the type we used to patronize. There are a few Chinese restaurants, which have steam tables, but no American cafeteria styles, in downtown Oakland.

Dee's Change of Employers

After Dee graduated from Medical Transcription School, she started looking for work. Dee had chosen the medical field, which does not have a large demand for that type of training. But I must say, the subject was very interesting, learning all the parts of the human body, and the names given to each part. I do not recall, but there must be thousands of parts. I do not know how anyone could know that much, but I am sure most doctors knew them at one time. Most doctors nowadays have specialized in one area of the body. I understand that! But we still have all of Dee's books, and occasionally I look at them. Dee worked hard, and studied hard. I have always been very proud of her accomplishments, no matter what they were.

Dee made a nice resume after school, but her experience was only in the food industry. and none in the medical field. She put her resume in probably 12-15 places. Our society did not have the Internet in 1977. She was able to work at a few nursing homes, for a day or two, but did not like them. She applied at two hospitals, but nothing permanent came up. We had been Kaiser (HMO) members since 1967, because of Dee's working as a waitress. These benefits were gained by the Waitress and Bartenders Union, and were our health care insurance benefits. Dee had chosen Kaiser Medical for herself, and me as her dependent. Kaiser Medical, was and still is a top notch Medical facility, and well known across the country. Dee suggested she wanted to put in her application at Kaiser, which she did.. Their facility here in Oakland, is large, has a large number of employees, and has thousands of members, and also has a lot of turnover of workers. Mostly because workers with different expertise in different fields, would be able to bid on jobs, if they had the qualifications, and therefore be able to move to a different department. Workers were constantly moving around to different departments, and some people were retiring too. Dee was trying to get employment, but only at any department she qualified for. In September of 1977, Jeff, a manager of the Central Appointments Department, called Dee, and said he had an opening in their department for a temporary receptionist. Because one of his staff had moved on to a different position, he felt Dee could fill that position when needed. Some workers would become pregnant, some quit, there were various reasons for employee changes. There were several men employees at Kaiser who wanted to make moves to other departments. Jeff called Dee in for an interview, and asked her why she wanted to get out of the food industry. Dee explained that she wanted weekends off, and her waitress field was shrinking. Weekly waitress work, Monday thru Friday, was becoming very scarce in downtown Oakland. Most waitress work required working weekends, especially dinner houses, who served cocktails. Dee never wanted any part of being a cocktail waitress. Jeff understood that but said that he did not feel comfortable hiring a person with no medical background, but he also said he would take a chance on Dee. Jeff had no way of knowing how hard a worker Dee was. Now Dee had a foot in the door. Jeff assigned Dee to work there in Central Appointments for the next 2 weeks, to learn the work that needed to be done. It did not take Dee long to learn and understand what the job requirements were.

After Dee had worked two weeks in Central appointments, she had learned the names of the other employees in that department, and the procedures for doing the work. Dee learned quickly about which people were good trainers. After the first two weeks, someone took time off, and Dee continued working the entire weekly schedule. I think Dee worked straight for about two months before the department was back to full staff, which meant Dee would need to stay home until there was another opening. All employees had to bid on a job in another department, if they wanted to get a different job. All jobs were filled by seniority, and qualifications.. Some employees in Central Appointments wanted to move around to different departments. Central Appointments was not a bad place to work, but most people wanted to learn more about the different departments and jobs, and wanted to move. I think Central Appointments was a starting point for some newer employees. There are many departments, and specialties within the medical field at Kaiser. New employees do not have any benefits until they are assigned to one department permanently, they have no earned time for sick leave, vacation, or medical benefits. After a few months of employment, there was an opening in a different department, and Dee applied for it. Jobs were posted for all employees to look at and bid on, and they were posted for only for a specific length of time. Another employee with a little more seniority received that specific position, instead of Dee.. Dee kept working in Central Appointments, but with no benefits, only beginning wages. Other job openings opened up, but Dee was not qualified for them.

After about another month, a job opened up in the Medical Clinic. Dee applied, and was awarded the new job. She was still on call, but she was now assigned to a department. Now she would be earning employment time, but not Medical benefits. Dee did her training, and learned the procedures. She did not have assigned hours, but called the night before if she was to come to work the next day. The manager usually told Dee during the day while she was working, that is, if they wanted her to come to work the next day. This department also assigned receptionists to the Emergency Room. Dee had to work the 2nd shift in the Emergency Room for a few months. Dee would ride the bus to work, and I would come and pick her up at the end of her shift. Being a receptionist was similar to waitress work, as you are always dealing with people. And Dee is a people person, and always has been, since I have known her. Dee liked being a receptionist.

Not long after Dee was assigned to the Medical Department, other workers moved on to different positions, and Dee ended up as a permanent employee in the Medical Department. Now Dee had full benefits. Dee enjoyed her work, and made friends with other employees. One special one was Charlie. Charlie was African american, crazy as can be, and he and Dee always had the clinic laughing. Charlie called Dee "Mom". It makes me laugh, just thinking about those two crazies working together. Some employees were nicer than others, and some were much better at their jobs than others. Dee liked working at Kaiser. After she had been working in this department for about 2 years, there was a need for an additional receptionist in the Psychiatry Department. The Psychiatry Department was small at that time, but the need for this type of medicine was getting greater, and the department was expanding. Kaiser Foundation was growing, and getting more and more members everyday. Psychiatry started with one full-time and one part-time doctor in this Department, with only one receptionist. As the Department grew, more doctors were hired, and more reception help was needed. Dee did not volunteer for the Psychiatry Department, she was basically drafted. Dee had the least amount of seniority of the receptionist crew. She never complained. She felt she had been chosen because of her personality, more so than her experience or qualifications. She learned the different doctors, and their different mannerisms, quirks, etc.. and the registration process for members requiring service. Some Psychiatric Doctors are very smart in their field, but sometimes I wonder about their common sense. This department was growing fast, and needed more space. Originally the department was on Piedmont Avenue, and had offices in some other office building spaces on Piedmont Avenue. This timeline was somewhere around the early 1980's.

As Kaiser grew, new people came to work in the Psychiatry

Department. Mary was already there, and Dee was now there, Carol moved to this department, Brenda also, and some others although I cannot recall their names. There were many other receptionists over the 24 years that Dee worked in the Psychiatry Department. Many more doctors were hired, Clinical Social Workers, nurses, etc. I cannot remember the titles of so many of them. Many of the psychiatrists, and other staff had lots of interests other than their field of work. Most of the doctors like to party a lot, and consume alcohol, good food, and have a good time off the job. They would celebrate many different things during the year, birthday parties, holidays, and any reason to have a get together. They really liked to party, and many of them knew the rules for partying! Their parties were always well organized. I think their job created some stress, and this was one way of handling that stress. No one became inebriated, but there was a lot of alcohol consumed. The parties would take place just about anywhere, parks, peoples houses, community rooms, restaurants, etc.. Some of the doctors' houses were gorgeous. And of course the reception crew was usually invited, maybe not all of them, but Dee was. They all really liked Dee, she was a fun person, and since she did not drive, I was usually invited too. I always tried to fit in. I knew nothing about the work they did. But I had opportunities to talk about common sense work, such as construction, buildings, remodeling, driving, travel, etc.. Those were a few. I have always enjoyed architecture, because I wanted to be an architectural designer. At some of the parties, we had some very good discussions about different buildings, and projects. Some of the doctors knew about the local famous architects, Julia Morgan especially, as she was from Berkeley, and a couple of others too. At these parties, it would give Dee and me a chance to socialize, dance, eat different kinds of foods, and just have a good time. They all gave Dee a great, "Really Great Retirement Party", and I mean a "Great Party". They were a fun group of people. We have remained friends with some of these Kaiser employees.

I used to take Dee to work in the mornings, and pick her up after work. It was something I wanted to do for her, I Loved her. And when I would be around the clinic, while waiting for her to finish her work day, I would have a chance to maybe say a greeting to other employees, and help them in any way I could. Dee would sometimes get discouraged about her work, but we would talk it over, and work it out. No place is perfect. If Dee had a tough day, for sure we would be eating our dinner out that evening. Dee's retirement benefits are great. Kaiser is and was good to both of us. One of the Psychiatry doctors was always jokingly accusing me of stalking Dee, and he was right!! I was able to joke along with many other employees too. Several people gave Dee little gifts over time, usually some type of toy kitty. There is one I want to mention. One of the Brink's Security Guards who usually picked up Kaiser's monies, gave Dee this really cute Tricky Cat. It was around Halloween time, and when you pressed the kitty's belly, it would meow, and vibrate all around. At first, it was a little scary, as it would catch people off guard, but people liked it. Everyone liked Dee, and she liked them. Dee acquired quite a few toy animals. She had a collection.

I believe it was 1987, when the Psychiatry Department moved from the Piedmont avenue location, to the King's Daughters Home. It is a Julia Morgan designed building on Broadway, in downtown Oakland, built around 1930. It had many more rooms, more space, meeting rooms, rooms to hold classes, and just more elbow space. That was about the time the department quickly started expanding. They also opened a Drug and Alcohol Clinic, a Child Care Clinic, mostly at other locations in Oakland. Kaiser added several classes to help people. Kaiser always had top notch people. They took good care of Dee and myself. We sincerely thank them all.

After Dee had been working for Kaiser Permanente here in

Oakland for about 26 years when, at 66 years of age, she retired. We had talked a lot about her retirement. And it just so happened, about this time, Kaiser was making some changes in their retirement plans. We looked over Dee's situation, and received estimates on her retirement pay and benefits. I wanted Dee to retire, but Dee did not want to retire. However, we found that she would lose a substantial part of her benefits if she remained working. So we put all the figures together, and we decided Dee would retire in January, 2004. Dee did retire, and they gave her a wonderful retirement party. Dee had been working since she was 14 years old, and I felt she deserved a rest. 52 years working seemed long enough. Dee had always been a very efficient employee for all the employers she had worked for. I had confidence Dee would find many things to keep her occupied. Dee did well with retirement, and we did many different things on the weekends. All through our marriage, we would eat out in restaurants at least 3 or 4 times a week, maybe more. We continued that same pattern. But I had been thinking that if I retired, we could do many more things together. And we have. Dee and I had talked about traveling to Europe, Canada, Mexico, New York City, and many other places. Retiring would give us time to do this. Also, my work was very physically demanding. The work was taking its toll on my body. I wanted to protect my aching body, and try to keep my health, so I retired in March of 2005. Those first months of retirement, I just rested. But it took me some time to adjust. I needed to get some professional help to adjust. Dee adjusted quickly to retirement, but I did not. I think I was just too regulated to getting up early, and doing physical work. But I always wanted to be with Dee, and care for her the best I could. All went well for some time, but then the Aalzheimer's disease set in. It has been tough, but I continue to try my best to keep Dee going, and myself too. Since Dee was diagnosed, I have learned a lot about this disease. And I personally have seen how it affects the people who may have it. We never know what tomorrow will bring for any of us. But Dee is, and always will be "The Love of my Life."

Dee's Other Interests

Dee and I loved to go to the county fairs. We were able to go to the California State Fair twice since we have lived here in northern California, but Sacramento gets very hot in August and September. Those are the months the fair is usually scheduled. Dee does not do well with the heat. At the fairs we usually did not go on the carnival rides, as we were never in for those kinds of thrills. Dee always wanted to see the baked goods, crafts, floral displays, etc. and we loved to look at the quilts, and different knitting exhibits. Inside the large display buildings were all kinds of things to look at and for sale. Some had many things school children made, and 4H exhibits. 4H exhibits are usually some types of articles young people may have made at their schools. Some examples are woodworking projects, knitting projects, baked articles, and sewing projects, etc.. There are also different animals, which were raised for 4H competitions too. They are usually judged by a knowledgeable person for each of their projects, or animals, which were entered into the competition. And many of their projects show some very highly talented young people . There are plenty of things to look at fairs, especially in the commercial buildings. Most of these items were for sale too. Fairs always have the very best food, maybe not very healthy, but good. We liked the sandwiches. And of course we had to have ice cream and candy. I don't remember what else we may have tried. County fairs usually have some good entertainment. I always wanted to look at the livestock, farm equipment, chickens, sheep, rabbits, etc.. Dee wanted to see them too. We always caught the art and photo exhibits. Years ago, I entered pictures in the county, and state fairs. We would check the art and photo exhibits to see which ones won. We would spend several hours just wandering around. Sometimes we played the horses. We went to county fairs in Pleasanton, CA., Vallejo, CA., Santa Rosa, CA., San Mateo, CA., etc.. The last few trips to the county fair in Pleasanton, I would place Dee in her transport chair, and I would push her around the fairgrounds. We always enjoyed all the fairs. Of course, San Francisco has its share of fair-like occasions going on frequently, too.

At the San Mateo County fair in 1985, Dee saw a piano she liked. Brand new, Schafer and Sons, a very nice one. We purchased it on time, and made payments. Credit cards were not in existence then, or if they were around, Dee and I did not have one. I did not know Dee had even thought of playing the piano. Dee's grandmother used to pound on her piano, and sing in the Lithuanian language, but really she did not know how to play the piano. The grandmother did this to wake up some of the family and it worked. Our new piano was delivered to our home a few days later. Dee signed up with a good teacher for lessons. It is hard to find a teacher who will teach adults. We old timers are harder to teach. Dee took lessons for a year, and then the teacher moved out of state. Dee found another teacher, but she really was not interested in teaching Dee. Dee does not have very much musical talent. If you have ever heard Dee sing, you may agree with me. But that does not mean I do not love her, we all do. Dee tried to play her piano, talent or little talent, and she is my girl, but eventually she gave up on the piano.. That piano has sat here in our house for all these years. After I retired, and probably about 2010, I decided I would try my luck at playing it. It is rewarding to play! I am not good, but I entertain myself. I took lessons for a couple years, and studied the books. I can put notes together that make sense. Dee always liked to listen to my efforts. Dee sang along on a few songs. I have a long way to go, but I do enjoy the piano. I wish Dee could have accomplished it, but she tried. But I love this girl, and what she does not have in musical talent, she has in love.

Church Services

When I was still in the Navy, in 1967, and while we lived in Alameda, we attended church services a few times. The Catholic Church was up the street in the next block. I knew Dee was a baptized Catholic, but I had never belonged to any church. We had left California for several months and when we moved back, we started attending the Catholic Church, not too regular at first. I remember, in July of 1970, after we moved to the rented house in Oakland, California, there was a Catholic Church about two blocks away. Dee always wanted both of us to go to church together. That was certainly OK with me. I have never intentionally stayed away from any church. When Dee said she wanted to go check out this church, I was all for it. We checked the marquee, to see the times for the services. The next Sunday, we walked up to this church. I knew it was a Catholic Church, and we went to this specific church about three times. Then Dee said she did not want to go to that church again. I asked why and Dee responded, "It is too Conservative". Of course, I had no idea what she was talking about. But Dee somehow checked around and we attended a couple other Catholic churches until she learned about the St Francis de Sales Cathedral Church in downtown Oakland. Dee liked this church, and I then realized what Dee meant by conservative. This church welcomed anyone, there were no dress requirements, you could just come in and listen and enjoy the message and services. On Sundays, it was packed with parishioners. We had found a church that Dee felt comfortable with and I liked it too. We started going to this church around 1972. Dee liked this church so much, we went every Sunday morning. We decided that we wanted to go to the early service, and then we would go to San Francisco for breakfast afterwards. Dee never received communion, nor I, because she said, we were not in good standing with the church. I did not know what that meant, but I found out later. We made friends with many others at this church, and became really good friends with some. There was a school there at first, but then it was torn down because of low attendance. Many people were moving out of Oakland, and out to the surrounding suburbs. Younger people could purchase property cheaper there, that is why the decline in children's attendance. Of course the Nuns taught at that school. This specific church had lots of music, great musicians, some from UC Berkeley, and a great choir. The priests always gave great messages, and sometimes church members acted the messages out in front of the altar. The services were always uplifting. After a few years, I was asked to be an usher, which I did not mind doing. I wanted to help anywhere I could. Everything was going along pretty well, until 1989. Then they asked me to be the head usher. I said I could not, as I was not a Catholic. The person talking to me about this position, head usher, told me I had to leave the church, and not attend anymore services because I was not a baptized Catholic. I did not feel very good about this, and I can still remember the look on that man's face, as he stood on the front steps, telling me I had to get out of that church. It seemed to me that everyone should be welcome at any church. But it just so happened, two great friends at that church were there at that moment. They did not know I had not been baptized to be in the Catholic Church, but they immediately said they would take care of that. They made arrangements to sponsor me, and have me baptized by the Bishop. These fellows were very active at this church. I attended classes for a year, and was baptized at Easter in 1990. I do not feel much different now than before, because I had received much information about the Church from Dee, but I now know the purpose of Communion. At the time I was Baptized, Dee was given recompense, and our marriage was Blessed, which now put us in good standing with the Catholic Church. I wanted to do this for Dee because I felt she was missing something. I now know what that was. I am happy to be a Baptized Catholic. I love that lady Dee! I would do anything for my Dee!

Some Catholic churches have fundraisers, for school support, etc.. Dee and I went to many of these. If an organization needed funds, we usually participated. We purchased tickets to raise the funds.needed. Many prizes were donated, and we donated some too. If I had the winning ticket, sometimes I would pass the prize on to the next person. Dee also won cosmetics, kitchen gadgets, etc. Dee is the lucky one, and it rubbed off on me. Dee would tell me to buy tickets, and then laugh at me when I won. She had me buying Irish Sweepstakes Tickets, and taking chances on most everything. I followed Dee, she is my Love. Dee's the gambler!

Food Serving, and Delivery

We attended this church every Sunday, and other activities on occasion. Usually on Sundays we volunteered at the dining room just down the street, the St Vincent de Paul dining room. The church we had been attending, also cooked and served Thanksgiving Day and Christmas Day dinners for anyone who wanted to eat, mostly low income people, shut-ins, and homeless people. I was usually the dishwasher, mostly pots and pans. We helped do this for a couple years, and then there was a need for drivers to take the meals to shut-ins. So Dee and I volunteered to do this. We would go to the church kitchen, pick up a list of people to visit, and collect the meals for them. We chose East Oakland mostly because most people did not want that area of town. We would take off, deliver the meals and talk briefly to each recipient. Some were in a terrible condition, and some lived in terrible conditions. We had to report some names to the authorities, because of their unhealthy, and unsafe living conditions. Then we would go back to the church to see if anything else was needed for us to do. The delivery process usually took us at least 2 hours. Sometimes it was necessary for us to take a second list for delivery, but we never minded as we were doing the work for God. Then, when we were all finished, Dee and I would go to San Francisco, to the St Francis Hotel restaurant, and we would have our Thanksgiving or Christmas dinner. The hotel restaurant was always open, not crowded because we were there before the crowd. It was always fun and delicious. The hotel restaurant had a Holiday Special for the season. Good food, good service, and we usually beat the crowds. Dee and I did not like crowds, we liked our privacy. We always had a good time with each other. This was our way, a kind of reward, for Dee and me to celebrate the holidays. Dee and I have always been lucky, we were in pretty good health at that time, and we could climb any stairs. Plus we could afford the time and money.

    This specific church which we attended suffered severe damage during the 1989 earthquake. We could not raise enough money to repair it, and as a result the church was torn down. Dee and I tried to help raise the 2 million dollars needed to repair it. A few years before, the school had been torn down, around 1980. The Diocese then built a small building for get-togethers, some school rooms for spiritual education and a kitchen, making a nice and quiet place. The church held services there for a while, after the earthquake. Then the services were moved to a different church down the street several blocks away. We hesitated to attend those services, because we were in the habit of going to church earlier on Sunday morning. We usually attended 8am services, and those services did not start until 10:30am. We also had other friends that felt the same way. This is when we all started attending a church in Alameda. We had been attending services at the torn down church for about 20+ years. We started attending church services in Alameda, and then we would all go out for breakfast afterward. This went on for only a few years, then a friend died, then a lady friend died, then another man friend died, and then the last lady friend died. That left Dee and me on our own. Dee and I had been attending this church in Alameda, for about 25 years. Dee and I just decided to remain with that specific church. I am happy to do anything with Dee. When Dee started to suffer from Alzheimer's disease, we were able to go to a different church on Saturdays, because they have a healing service and the people recognize that sick people do make uncontrollable noises. It is a very nice church, and has had several activities over the years which we have participated in to raise money for different reasons. Now that Dee suffers more from Alzheimer's disease, we are not able to attend any church, because of the disease. Dee usually makes too much noise. We cannot have that noise, when people are trying to pray. Due to Dee's medical condition, Dee and I are unable to attend any church services now. But I hope we can return soon.

Meditation

In the late 80's, Dee had seen an advertisement for Transcendental Meditation. An Indian Spiritual leader started this type of meditation in this country. It was to help people to meditate, and help the relaxing process for individuals. It was basically to help reduce the stress we accumulate in our bodies. Yes, spiritual, because you start with a mantra, which you concentrate on, and repeat over and over; this is recommended for approximately 20 minutes. It was very helpful, especially when stress is a major part of a person's day, usually caused by work.

We attended the classes for a short period of time, and then felt we had sort of learned what to do. It worked very well, and we meditated consistently for about two years. It was very hard to do, early in the morning: first we needed to get up a half hour early each day, to attend to all our necessary duties before going to work and still allow time to meditate. And I must confess that I would fall asleep much too often, while saying the mantra, because I was still tired from the previous day's necessities, overwork being the main problem. This went on for some time, and we also meditated at night as well. After about two years of meditating, my job changed at Del Monte, and I had to start earlier in the morning for work. I would drop Dee off at the bus stop in Alameda, for Dee to take the bus to her work. She would get there early. The bus dropped Dee off in front of her workplace. Dee never drove a vehicle, so I always looked out for her transportation as best I could, and she did not mind riding the buses. It later turned out that I would take Dee to work, and pick her up in the evenings after our work was finished for the day. I always tried to look out for Dee, and make sure she was safe. But one day, after Dee had acquired the drop foot, and as she was getting on the bus, she fell backwards off the step of the bus. Luckily there was a gentleman directly behind her, waiting to board the bus. He caught her, and kept her from falling. It would have been a disaster if she had fallen. She thanked the man profusely for his efforts. I saw what happened, because I always waited for Dee to enter the bus. But I was standing toward the back of the bus, and there was no way I could have caught her. I had never imagined anything like this happening, but it did. The drop foot has caused Dee to fall so many times. But as this did happen, I decided we had to make some more changes. I thought about what I could do. I decided I would take Dee to work, and pick her up after work. It might make Dee wait for me, or I might have to wait for her. This might cause our day to start earlier, but that was okay. No matter,

Dee's safety was more important than anything else. And Dee definitely was worth the extra time it took over the years for her to wait for me, and for me to wait for her. So our Transcendental Meditation sort of went by the wayside, because of the changes we needed to make.

About 1995, after we had started attending the church in Alameda with our other friends, as we were leaving the church, Dee saw an item hanging on the bulletin board at the back of the church for Spiritual Meditation. It was called Hesed Community, and was run by Sister Barbara. Sister Barbara had studied the Benedictine philosophy, and had started this type of Community on her own. She must have started it a couple years before we started attending. It was, and is very lovely, and helpful in many many ways. It always starts by reading a phrase from the Bible, a meaningful verse, then we think about what those words mean to each of us silently. After a few moments of silence, we are allowed to express the words, or phrases, which may have touched us. Then there would be about twenty minutes of Mediation, either using the mantra, Maranatha, or people could use their own mantra. Very flexible. It was for all different religions. We attended as often as we could, but mostly on Monday evenings. The community meetings were close to our home here in Oakland. There were other Hesed activities during the year that Sister had set up. They were spiritual in nature and there was usually music involved. Sister had written most if not all the music herself. She had been a school teacher, and a pianist in her earlier years. Over the years, we became good friends. The three of us often went out to dine at different restaurants, always good food. Sister Barbara gave me piano lessons for a while. She was a very, very good teacher, and would make sure I knew what I was doing with the music. Sister Barbara was a perfectionist, and taught me how to play the piano correctly. To this day, I am still trying to perfect the music she played so very well. Dee would sit and watch, and sometimes sing along with us, to the songs we were playing. Sister Yvone joined us on occasion. After a while I was able to conquer some songs pretty well. This went on for a few years, until Dee developed Alzheimer's, and we could no longer attend Hesed Mediations. But we were all able to eat out together for a little while after Dee had been diagnosed. Then sadly enough, Sister Barbara developed Alzheimer's herself, and is now living in a care center. Hesed Community is still in existence, and has a few members, and we do our best to try to contribute to the Community financially. I wish we could still be involved, but with Dee's medical situation, it would be impossible. She cannot sit still, and could never be quiet. And with Dee's current mobility, it would be next to impossible, because Dee cannot walk.

Dee and I liked to Eat Out

As I have mentioned many times, Dee and I, all through our life together, ate out in restaurants frequently. Probably the most was when there were restaurants still remaining in downtown Oakland, sort of like cafeteria style. Those were our favorites. The amazing thing about those memories was the people we encountered over the time. We did not maintain a personal relationship with any of them, but there were people we liked and talked with. Just a few dining place's: Manning's Cafeteria, Cafe Lido, Merritt restaurant, Elegant Farmer, Senor Nero's, Pier 29, Brekke's Cafeteria. And so many many more. Brekke's cafeteria was a great place to eat, it was family owned. The father did the cooking, the mother collected the money and the children took the orders, served the food, and cleaned up: a great family and atmosphere. We often drove to Stockton, to eat at the Olde Hoosier Inn. The owner had started this restaurant in the 40's or 50's, as the family had migrated there from Indiana. The atmosphere was the old antique style, and there were many, many antiques. The food was very good, but probably had lots of calories. We also drove to San Jose to the 94th Squadron and many, many times we drove to the Coffee Tree, and Nut Tree in Vacaville, California. We went to the Fairmont hotel in SF, Sears in SF, St Francis Hotel in SF, and so many more, probably a hundred that we dined at over time. All usually had some type of favorable atmosphere and food. The reason I am saying this is because we were able to make many solid decisions over these conversations, as we used to dine and talk. Dee did 80% of the talking, and I did the listening. I always liked the subjects, and I would get so many different ideas, plus I liked to listen to Dee talk. When Dee talked, she was like a professor, she could get her points across. And if there was some kind of problem, we would talk it out. I think this is why we never argued. We alway talked things out, and came to some type of conclusion. No, not everything was perfect, nor did everything work out, but we were always able to come to a satisfactory decision which we both agreed on. If Dee could mention the different restaurants now, I probably could tell you what food was our favorite at that specific eating establishment. Some were dinner houses, and some were sandwich shops. We never went hungry, but as I have said, if the food was not great, we never went back. Oh, so many, many memories! And ironically, Mr Brekke, who owned Brekke's Cafeteria, lives close to us. He sold the cafeteria many years ago. Mr Brekke just celebrated his 101st year old birthday!

Dee's Coffee

When I met Dee, she was a coffee-holic. She drank 6, 7 or more cups a day and at night too: caffeine never bothered her. She lived on coffee. I never drank coffee (I called it burnt water), not even while I was in the Navy, but Dee used to make it, and I got so I would drink some. As we ate out in restaurants, we almost always ordered coffee to drink, mostly because restaurants always have it ready, and you can get as many refills as you want. But I got so I liked it, and it had no calories. Dee would probably still be hooked on it, if it was not for her illness. She probably acquired the coffee habit from working in restaurants. But I remember Dee telling me that when she was about 5 years of age, her grandmother would give her a cup of milk, and then add a few drops of coffee to it. Well, Dee thought she was a big girl by being able to drink coffee. Dee's grandmother was very, very proud of Dee, she called her Dorikky, which must have been a Lithuanian name. And when her father came home from work, Dee would tell him she was a big girl, and had been drinking coffee. John would laugh, put Dee on his shoulders, and run around the house with her. John would be singing the song "How I Love The Kisses of Dolores". Dee' father adored Dee, until he met the step-mother. Then, when Dee's real mother died, and the father remarried the step-mother, everything changed, and drastically. Dee's happy life ended when Dee was taken away from her grandmother Palaskas. The coffee is probably why Dee only weighed 103 pounds when we were married. Dee drank her coffee instead of eating. But I know Dee has always been an attractive lady. Many people, who come into our house, and look at our pictures of Dee, they usually remark about how attractive Dee is and was. Dee is such a beautiful person!

Remembering some of the stories Dee has told me about her

family, I can remember one along with the coffee. When Dee was little, she, her father, and grandmother went to church every Sunday morning. They walked to church, as it was only about 2 blocks away. Then after church, they would stop at a bakery, and pick up fresh, hot donuts, and take some home to eat along with their Sunday morning breakfast. Sometimes I guess, they ate a lot of donuts with their breakfast. Kids at that age love to eat donuts, I know I did. Donuts were a very big treat for Dee, because money was scarce. Dee told me of some of the things her grandmother Marcella made. I believe Marcella made bread, and probably made a lot of other baked goods, Lithuanian style. Kugeli was a favorite, made from potatoes. And other dishes that I do not know. We were able to make many solid decisions over these conversations. I do not know the names of the dishes, but they were mostly made from potatoes too. Dee told me that a lot of potatoes were grown in Lithuania. Marcella probably made a lot of potato soup. Dee said Marcella had a vegetable garden in the backyard, along with flowers too. And Dee said Marcella always had a pot of coffee on the stove. This is probably why Dee always liked drinking coffee. Marcella must have spent most of her day preparing food when the children were still at home. And Dee said the family lived in the kitchen all the time. I am sure this big stove was very important to everyone, especially in the winter to stay warm.. Dee said she would sit on a chair behind this big stove, to keep warm during wintertime, and watch Marcella prepare food. Sometimes, Marcella and Dee would sit together on chairs, and put their feet in the stove's oven to warm them in the winter.

 I feel this is important to talk about at this point in the book. I have mentioned the kitchen, and the big stove, back in earlier pages. But I wanted to explain that this kitchen was a big part of Dee's childhood memories. This is the only area of memories I could get Dee to talk about, memories about an activity in the big kitchen. This kitchen somehow was a big part of Dee's earlier life. Dee would tell me about Marcella preparing food, and laughing. I never knew, but I imagine Marcella had Dee help her some. Of course the big stove was their heater in the winter time. And the big table had lots of room. The family ate together at this big table, and that is where Pete would send his coffee flying. I am sure many other things happened in this kitchen when Dee was a little girl. She talked about Aunt Marion, John, Pete, Marcella, and Dee eating together. These memories in the big kitchen must have been the main memories that Dee wanted to keep. Dee only mentioned the kitchen, and the church she attended.

Dee's grandfather worked in the coal mines, and probably did not make much salary. Dee never said much about her grandfather Pete, except for the sending of the coffee via spoon to the receiving kid at the table and about the distance, and lack of love between Marcella and Pete. This would have been around 1940.

Thinking about sweets, over the years, Dee and I stopped frequently at the Merritt bakery, and restaurant, a very popular establishment here in Oakland. Dee and I would bring home some pastries for ourselves and we ordered cakes for different occasions. After we moved here on Rosedale, there was a Portuguese bakery close by, a really good bakery. Dee liked to sleep in on Saturdays if she could. Earlier in our presence here on Rosedale, on most Saturday mornings, I would walk down, purchase pastries, and bring them home for us to eat. Fresh warm goodies have a lot of rewards. Calories? Oh, how we loved the pastries I brought home, very fresh. We both had no weight problem at that time, and did not for many years. But as time went by, we both gained weight. I could lose it with not much of a problem, but Dee always had trouble starving herself to lose her extra pounds. The Portuguese bakery is gone now, a Mexican grocery store replaced it. Now that Dee has Alzheimer's disease and I have started doing the preparation of meals, she has gained weight. I have baked too much, fed her portions that are too big, had to give her Ensure, etc.. Dee would be better if she could lose a few pounds. I have cut back on the portions I feed her. But I cannot starve her, she is the woman I have always loved, and always will. I will keep trying to help her lose weight.

Hair Stylists

Dee was born with beautiful red hair, and lots of it too, very thick, in 1937, in Scranton, Pa.. Dee's mother was a first generation American from Irish immigrants. Dee's father was a first generation American from Lithuanian immigrants. When I met Dee, she always fixed her hair herself. And it usually took her about 2 hours every morning. Dee would tease it up somehow, with a comb. I watched her many times, no way I could ever do that! But Dee's hair always looked fabulous!! It would look sort of like an upside down bee hive nest. A sample is in our wedding picture. It truly was a work of art. I never knew who Dee's hair dresser was before I met her, but after we moved to Oakland, she began looking for a hair stylist. Dee was working as a waitress at the time. She decided to look for a stylist to cut and fix her hair which would be close to downtown. Dee tried a few places, but was not happy with any of them. Then she tried a stylist who was a patron of the restaurant where she worked. Sam was his name; he was an immigrant from Scotland. Sam was really good, Dee liked his work, but then Sam decided to move back to Scotland, so Dee found another good stylist, Andy. Andy was good, and had done movie stars' hair, and other professionals too. Very unusual styles at times. At first Dee liked his work, but after a while, she became discouraged with it. Dee has such unusual hair, and he would keep experimenting with designs that Dee did not like. Some she liked, but many she did not care for. And so many of his styles were hard for her to care for by herself. He was pricey and Dee could not afford to go to him every day like the stars could do. After a while Dee was looking for someone else to care for her hair. Then Dee asked the wife of one of my co-workers at Del Monte about the stylists she liked. The lady recommended a man named Gary, who was here in downtown Oakland, close by, and said she liked his work. Dee made an appointment with Gary, liked his styling and cuts, and has been going to Gary for about 45 years now. Everybody comments on Dee's hair, especially when it is styled pretty. Dee has always had many compliments about her hair. It is always beautiful, fixed up or not! Dee's hair has now turned blondish in color, typical of red haired people. But her hair still has a little red on the sides, usually visible when washing it. Dee has always been a natural redhead; many ladies have tried to copy Dee's natural hair color. Dee's grandmother used to make it look like Shirley Temple's curls and Dee's father John, would put her on his shoulders, and run around the house. John was also very proud of Dee's hair. This made Dee so happy, because Dee adored her father. But one other thing about Dee's hair: Dee never liked to be called "Red". I respected her wishes and never called her "Red". I defended Dee, defended her even when some one would make a remark about her behind her back. I defended Dee, no matter what the situation. Dee is her name, and not "Red" I would say. Some dirty old man asked me one time, if Dee was a natural redhead. I never said anything, I felt that was insulting, and did not deserve a response.

Dee's Green Thumb

Dee has always liked flowers and tried to keep several growing, but she just did not have a green thumb at all. Because I adored Dee, numerous times, weekly mostly, I would bring home fresh cut flowers for her. Dee has many vases, and would place the vases with the cut flowers in them on our tables. She liked them so very much. Many people over time brought potted flowers for her as gifts. House plants usually have growing directions, and tell how to care for the plant. Dee would put them on a table and water them, but they usually ended up dying. I tried to tell her how to care for them, but it did not work very well. Dee watered too much, or not at all, but I think she forgot. But Dee tried!! Now, I take care of all the flowers that we have in the house, and outdoors. When we had the pussy willow tree, I would bring in branches when it was in bloom. We had many other flowers, and I would bring in stems and cuts. Flowers can be expensive to let die, and I wanted to keep the flowers that had been given to Dee alive and blooming. I don't like to see plants die, unless it's the end of their growing season. When we moved here, we brought along a purple bougainvillae that we had at the other house. Since then, we have added many more flowers. We have roses, which I cut and bring in the blooms. We also have a gardenia from which I pinch off the blooms, bring them in and put them in a little dish. They have such a beautiful aroma. Our gardenia bush is in front of our front porch. When it is in its blooming period, the front porch has such a wonderful aroma, especially at night, and the aroma seeps into our living room. We still have some violets, cacti, and orchids, in our house and outside we have different kinds of orchids, Hoya's, more different kinds of cactus, Calla lilies, a lilac bush, geraniums, and a vegetable garden. We have always had many plants. Being raised on a farm, I like to see things grow and flourish. And I love to see the look on Dee's face when she sees them. Dee used to make a fuss over the fresh blooms I would bring in, and the aroma. She is very appreciative. I know she likes them.

When we moved here, the back yard had a pussy willow bush that grew taller than the house. It got so big that it was affecting the garage roof, and the bush started rotting on the inside. I had never seen a pussy willow tree grow so big. I had to cut it down, and haul it to the dump. Dee always liked Gravenstein apples, so I planted what was supposed to be a dwarf Gravenstein apple tree. But it turned out to be a full sized tree. It had lots of apples, but it got so very big, it was on top of the garage roof and raising the walkway, and it might have caused sewer problems. It would have ruined the foundation of the garage too. I had to cut it down and haul it to the dump. We then had a peach tree, but it died of peach leaf curl disease. We also had a beautiful lemon tree. It was getting pretty big, and it was next to our bougainvillea plant that runs across our backyard. Because our neighbor never took care of their property, they have rats. The rats came to our backyard, and nested in the lemon tree, and bougainvillea bush. So I had to cut both the lemon tree and bougainvillea down, and haul them to the dump. But now we just have a lilac bush, the bougainvillea which grew back, 2 dahlia trees, and a vegetable garden. I collect water from the roof above my radial arm saw. Radial arm saws are used for the cutting of wood. They usually require a large amount of space to house them. And they produce a large amount of sawdust when using them. With it outside, it is much easier to clean up the extra sawdust. I have made several things for Dee with this one. Dee suggested years ago for me to make benches. I did. We sold some, and gave many away. Dee even took two to Kaiser, for use in their work area. And the water I collect from the roof above this saw during the winter, I use to water most of these plants when summer comes. Out front, we have three Jade plants, and the gardenia bush. We have had other types of plants over the years, but for now this is what we like the best. And they are easy to care for, and use very little water. As I have aged and grown more tired of cutting and pruning, we have settled for more simple and easy to care for plants. I never water the lawns. They dry up during the summer and turn brown. Water here is precious, so I try to use very little. When I catch rain water over the winter, I store it in plastic garbage cans for summer use. I keep them covered to keep mosquitoes away.

Inside the house, we only have normal house plants. That's about it at present. When someone gives us a plant, I try to keep it growing and blooming. Dee always liked anything that bloomed. I used to bring home fresh flowers for Dee, but now, I just bring in Calla lilies, rose blooms, gardenia blooms, or whatever we may have with an open bloom, from our own flowers. And of course the garden always produces its own rewards, such as tomatoes, green beans, radishes, onions, chard, carrots, corn, beets, and probably more that I cannot recall. And lots of sunflowers.

Entertainment

Dee and I used to go to the Paramount Theater here in Oakland. Over the years we have seen many movies, many performances by numerous talents, dance programs, ballets, plays, musicals, etc., Victor Borgie being one of our favorites. The Paramount used to have old movie nights, and the cost was $5 per person to get in. They played the classics, mostly from around the 40's, and other classics of more recent times. They would advertise them on their marquis, and the movies were once a month. If it was a popular classic, there would be quite a crowd. We often found people Dee worked with or a few other people we knew. We all had the old classic movies in common. We took other friends with us sometimes. It was something really fun to do. Dee loved this so very much. We loved the Paramount Theater. It is a beautiful building, Julia Morgan was one of the Architects and designers. It was the top nightlife place in Oakland. Many programs go on there now, but we are physically unable to attend. I wish we could go there now. We used to go to San Francisco, and enjoyed several plays, opera's, musicals, and other entertainments, etc.. It was wonderful to experience the talents, and storytelling of the many different venues. We also loved to go to street fairs, both in Oakland and San Francisco. We probably purchased many things which we did not need. Yes, we went to other cities for this type of entertainment several times. Over the years, we saw many top named talents. I am not sure if anyone remembers: Beach Blanket Babylon?

Dee and I went to the Cow Palace in San Francisco two times, to see the Neil Diamond concert. We also saw Neil Diamond twice here in Oakland. Neil Diamond was probably the most loved musician for Dee. Neil Diamond was from the New York/ New Jersey area. We both loved Neil Diamond's music. We also went to the Cow Palace many times to see dog shows, and cat shows. It is pretty easy to drive and park there. Going to downtown San Francisco for the different shows, the parking sometimes could be very difficult.

Dee also loved Bluegrass music. There used to be a pizza place here in Oakland's Rockridge area. Each weekend, on Friday nights, live bluegrass music was performed. One of my coworkers at Del Monte also liked bluegrass music and he told me about this. Dee and I would meet his family at the pizza place, order pizza, and enjoy the evening. We made many requests for different songs. Dee really likes Bluegrass Music. Sadly, my coworker died at an early age. They had children and to this day, I am able to see their son. He works at a restaurant. Of course, the pizza place is gone, and there is not much bluegrass music around here in Oakland, but San Francisco has a big Bluegrass Festival once a year. We have never gone to the show, as it is very crowded, but we do get to hear some of the songs being played. We would go, if we could, but it is extremely crowded.

Dee's Socializing

In the late summer of 2006, my godson's fiance was having her bridal shower, at her friend's house, in Turlock, California. Dee had been invited, and of course, I wanted Dee to attend. It must have been about 100 miles from our home here in Oakland. I drove Dee there that day. Dee had taken a gift, I do not remember what it was. It was a pretty warm day. A very nice place for her shower. We really like this young lady very much. I checked with the lady when we arrived, as to when I should come back to pick up Dee. Seems like it was in about three hours. I had remembered, from past golf outings, that close by was a great golf practice facility. So I spent my time usefully, by practicing my golf skills. For sure, I needed lots of practice. About the time I was told to be back to pick up Dee, I was there. Then the ladies wanted to feed me. I ate some really good food, and then Dee and I were on our way home. It was a wonderful day for visiting, and a great reason, and wonderful people. This young lady and my godson have been married for almost 14 years now. They have two children. She is a nurse, very knowledgeable about medicine and a true asset to the Medical Community. I call and talk to her about Dee's condition and any problems which occur. She is so very helpful. We love her, and her family very much.

Casinos

And another thing that Dee and I had the most fun at, was going to the Indian Casinos. We loved the scenery, a beautiful drive, and we stopped at anything along the way that appeared interesting, and we enjoyed each other's company. It is only about a 90 minute drive to get there. I loved doing this with Dee. Dee was pretty lucky, we both were lucky at winning or breaking even. We always had a system, only ours. Dee had suggested it, for gambling. I would put $300 in my right pants pocket, that was our gambling money. Then any winnings from any machine or other wager would go into my left pocket. We usually sat side by side, or Dee stood behind me and watched. We usually played one machine, sometimes two, because that was our best way of having fun when we gambled. Yes, I played Keno, and other games, but I could not include Dee when playing those. We played Roulette and Black Jack a little, but we were not very lucky. So we pretty much played the dollar machines. We loved the wheel of fortune machines. Never won much, but we had fun. It never mattered if we won much or not. Of course we wanted to win, that is the object, but we always managed to have fun. We laughed a lot. As long as I was with Dee, I was happy. And when the right pants pocket became empty, we stopped gambling. Then we would cash in the coupons, and all the coins from the machines. Then those profits would be put in my left pocket and to be kept there. That was our bank for our next trip. We never won much, but many times we had more in the left pocket, than we originally had in the right pocket. This method of gambling was Dee's doing, I may not have been so disciplined. We stopped gambling then, until our next trip. After we cashed in, we would eat at one of the good sit down restaurants. I always kept traveling and spending money separately in my wallet. After eating we would use the restroom then head for home. Many times we stopped on the way home; something else may have caught our eye and we would stop to check it out. Along the drive through the Capay Valley were fruit and produce stands. We purchased good fruits and vegetables on these trips. If we had been lucky at the casino, we would buy a lottery ticket at one of the little stores in that area. However, we never won much on any of those tickets.

Casinos are usually crowded on the weekends. If we were going to the Indian Casino, on a Saturday, we would leave our house early in the morning. It would be dark, but we could see the scenery, and anything interesting, on the way home. Our trips usually require most of the day. We normally only spent about three hours at a casino, then we would leave. But we did stay overnight a few times. Even then, we only spent a few hours gambling. At first, we could not afford to lose any of the $300 gambling money. But we would work together, and would get the pot of money back, and then away we would go again. We always worked together no matter what we were doing and we always had fun. Dee is my love.

When we were at the casinos we usually wanted to try all kinds of machines. Sometimes we were lucky, but we never won anything big. Most of the time when playing these different kinds of machines, Dee would stand behind, or beside me, then she could see exactly what was happening with that machine. Many times, Dee would tell me to double or triple up. Sometimes that worked and sometimes it did not work out. But Dee was my partner! We had fun.

When Dee and I went to Reno, Nevada, we stayed overnight, and sometimes two or three days. I almost always played a round of golf, at some golf course around the Reno area. Dee stayed in the room to read, or to check out the local stores and shops, etc.. When I came back from golf, we might have gambled a little, always using our system. Dee and I just enjoyed each other's company. And one time, Janet called, and said she and her husband Kurt were going to be in Reno and would like to meet us there if we could. Yes, we would meet them there, and we did. At that time, we owned the time share. We all stayed at the time share. It was roomy, plenty big enough for probably eight people. The four of us gambled a little, talked a lot, and enjoyed visiting. While in that area, Bill Clinton was making a speech about Hillary's run for the White House. We had to wait in line for three hours to get into the Reno Convention Center where he was to speak. There was no charge to get in to hear him. Bill gave a beautiful speech. Now, I understood the magnetic draw he had on people. He knew how to draw attention to the cause. Bill was a very good speaker, he surprised me. As we know, Hillary did not win the White House. But we were happy to see him, and hear him speak. That was the closest any of us had ever been physically to a politician. Bill spoke for about half an hour. The one thing I remember specifically about that trip was when we all went to Circus Circus Casino for breakfast the following morning. We sat down and ordered our food. I also liked to play Keno while eating. I chose a Keno ticket, picked my numbers and gave it to the Keno runner. Our food came, the runner brought my copy of the ticket back, and we proceeded to eat. I was watching the Keno board as the end of that specific Keno game ended. I looked at my ticket, checked my numbers, and I thought I had won $800.00. But I did not say anything to Dee, or Janet or Kurt. I caught the Keno runner, showed him the ticket, and said, "Did I win what I think I may have won?" He checked the ticket, and sure enough, I had won $800.00. What Luck!! Of course, I paid for our breakfast, and gave the Keno runner a $50.00 tip. Dee and I were happy to come home with a little profit. And my Dee says, "What did you do"? I then explained. She was proud of me. I really love this girl!!

    Many years ago, at least 40, Dee suggested I take a day off from work, and go to Reno. Every day there is a bus which leaves Oakland about 8am and goes to Reno, Nevada. This would be strictly a gambling bus. The casinos in Reno used to give each gambler coupons to enable us to get some money back from the cost of the trip, with food and drink coupons too. The bus would be in Reno for about 7 to 8 hours, and then return back to Oakland. It usually returned around 10 or 11pm. Most of the time the bus had approximately 35 passengers. Some gamblers won a small amount, but it sounded like most people lost most of their money. I did okay, but I never won much. But it was certainly something different from going to work. Dee always hoped I would come back a big winner. This makes for a long day. But I also hoped to bring back a large amount for Dee, you never know, when it comes to gambling. I tried to win the best way I could.

About 1973, Dee was working at the Ideal Coffee Shop in downtown Oakland. Next door to this coffee shop was an athletic apparel store. The owner of this store came into the coffee shop to eat and mentioned to Dee that he was looking for gamblers to go to Las Vegas. He had some kind of an agreement with a casino there, for him to charter a passenger plane to fly from Oakland to Las Vegas, and return after about 10 hours. The cost was $300 up front, and then when you arrived at the casino, they would give you the $300 back. Of course the casino thought each gambler would use it, and lose it in their casino. There were not any set rules though. The $300 was my usual gambling pot. I made this trip two times. The first time I lost most of my $300. Las Vegas is usually tight to win. The second time I went, after I got my $300, I played some machines and I hit $165. I still had most of my $300. I decided I did not want to lose any of my pot, so I put all the money I had from the gambling in my pocket, and I went outside and sat on a sidewalk bench, until it was time for the plane to depart to Oakland. I remember calling Dee, and telling her my plans. I never knew why Dee wanted me to try this, I think she just wanted to help the athletic store owner find gamblers. Dee was really the gambler. Dee hoped I would win, but I know she always said I was lucky. Dee thought for a long time that I was going to win something big, and so did I. I tried. I think the plane usually had about 25 passengers. It was different, but nothing I could fall in love with.

I think Dee was truly the real gambler. But each time we went gambling, she wanted me to do the playing. She always felt that I was luckier than she was. Over the years, Dee would tell me to buy chances on this or that. And I must confess, I won many prizes over the years, many bottles of wine, kitchen gadgets, coupons for restaurants, etc.. I took chances on most anything. I was pretty lucky at the casinos. It was true because I won $1,000.00 a few times. This is usually why my left pocket had more in it than my right pocket. Dee had me in the New York Lottery, when it was legal, and I was also in the Australian Lottery for a while. As luck would have it, we did win a little at both of them. But that was a long time ago, when out of state gambling was legal. Sending gambling issues via mail is now illegal.

Now, we only play the Lottery. We have never won much with the lottery, but we keep trying. It only takes one time winning, to make it worthwhile. Maybe someday! Dee has always supported my gambling, I have never gone crazy! I wish I could have won big, it would have made Dee so very happy. But Dee is my girl!

Golf Outings

For several years, starting in the late 90's, Dee and I used to go to Gualala, California. It is a little town north of San Francisco, next to where the Gualala River meets the ocean. I suppose 200 to 300 people may live there. There are 2 or 3 small hotels there, a few shops, and a couple grocery stores. There are some very good restaurants nearby as well as at the hotels. Because it is along the ocean, it must have had fishing businesses there at one time. The restaurants serve fresh seafood, but I do not know where they get their supply. I never saw any fishing boats. About a mile down Highway One is a place called Sea Ranch. It also is a place where people can rent a weekend or vacation home. A very nice place, although a little pricey. They also have a very good restaurant. Dee and I stayed there one time. Dee and I usually stayed in a hotel, they were much cheaper. There is also a great golf course there too. People who used to live in San Francisco sponsored a golf tournament there each year. They invited me for several years. It is a great course, but tight, with many sloping fairways, and lots of shrubbery type areas, plenty of trouble for a golfer. It's not a long course, but it's difficult. It sets along to the ocean. The group played several other golf challenge games. It was a nice group of players. And after golf, sometimes we met at a restaurant for dinner. The whole event took place over the weekend, we had a lot of laughs, and sometimes sorrows!! It depended on how well one played at the golf course. Dee usually wandered around the little town, shopped for trinkets, etc. Sometimes Dee would meet up with the other wives of golfers. After golf, I would come back and talk with Dee to see what she had discovered. Usually we would eat, go back to our room, relax, and maybe watch a little TV. We always went there on Friday morning, played a round of golf on Friday afternoon, and again on Saturday, and came home on Sunday. It was a fun and enjoyable outing. And Dee loved looking around, shopping, and relaxing, along with seeing all the new, and unusual sights. Dee and I loved doing this type of activity. When I retired from my last job, they gave me a gift certificate for a two day stay at Sea Ranch facility. It really is a great vacation escape.

    This was almost the same type of outing that had become a sort of common thing for Dee and me to do. We went to San Juan Batista, California, and other areas of northern California. I would golf, Dee and I would stay at a hotel. Usually Dee would read while I was at golf. She made friends with some of the ladies. Then after golf, we would find some place to eat, relax in our room and travel on the next day. We did this similar trip several times, at many different golf courses. We made several trips to the Central Valley of California. We made a few trips to the Sierra Mountain Foothills. We even went to Reno, Nevada after some outings. We made several trips to the Monterey, California area too. I loved golf, and Dee liked relaxing and reading and seeing all the different scenery. The only problem was, it could get pretty hot around the foothills of California, easily 100 degrees, and sometimes hotter in the summertime. Dee never liked the heat but most places have air conditioning there and we had air conditioning in the car. Monterey was Dee's favorite, it almost always has cool weather there.

Retirement

I have mentioned before that Dee retired in January, 2004. I retired in March of 2005. We did not have much extra money at first, because my income was reduced from my working salary to my pension. It took about 2 years for me to get our finances arranged, to where all the money would work best for us. Dee's salary and Social Security pay has not changed much over the years. She has gotten the cost of living increased. At first, I only had my California Public Employee's income. After a short time I signed up for my Del Monte Retirement, and a few months later I signed up for my Social Security Income. Over the years, my cost of living has increased. I could not draw from my IRA's, at first, not until I reached 70 years and six months of age, that is, I was not old enough. Dee did have a couple IRA's, but they were very small, and we cashed them in shortly after she retired. I started drawing from my IRA accounts after I reached the qualifying age, because I was required to do this. The IRA's are all in my name now, but they have always belonged to both Dee and myself, fifty fifty, because we both sacrificed to reach that goal, and I always explained this to Dee. She knew and she has always trusted me. Our retirement finances have worked out fairly well. The only problem is, Dee's health is now not well enough for us to do much anymore. I feel so very sad for Dee, she does not deserve this medical condition, Dee is a wonderful person. Dee would love to do things, and to see the sights again. And Dee loved to travel too. Dee always packed more than we needed, when we traveled.

The Dreaded Diagnosis

While I was working in 2004, when I would come home after work, Dee would tell me she was having a hard time remembering names. This is really when Alzheimer's disease was beginning. I did not think much about it, as I thought she was having senior moments, which is common among us seniors. I tried to keep a closer watch on Dee, and her memory as best I could. But I always had to keep an eye on her, as she frequently could lose things. She misplaced things all her life, but this was getting a little worse. But I still kept thinking this would pass. So then I retired in March of 2005. We always liked going to Monterey, and casinos, and just getting out to see the different scenery. I especially tried to get her out every weekend while I was still working. I did not want her to get bored or depressed. But as time went along, especially after I retired, I was totally aware of Dee's thinking and how she processed things. As we traveled, she did not seem to take as much interest in the scenery, she fell asleep often while I was driving. Dee was just not the same person after I retired. Dee did not seem to care anymore about going to Monterey, it was always her favorite spot to visit, that whole area. I could see that when we went to the casinos, Dee would only gamble with me by her side, and then, after some time, she would just watch me. The last two times we went to a casino, she would not play any machines and it did not seem as though she was interested at all in being there. Always before, she would be excited, full of life, and many times, want to stay overnight, which we did on occasion. Dee's progress of memory loss spanned about 10 years. Yes, I was aware, but somehow thought it all would pass. But what could I do? Many more years have now passed, and Dee's disease has taken a heavy toll on her. It has been a very sad, sad thing to watch.

In the middle of 2006, we went to see Dee's regular medical doctor. I thought she might be having problems which could be related to a medical or physical problem. Her doctor examined her, did blood work, etc. and did not see anything unusual. The doctor then referred her to the Neurology Department. We went to see the Neurology Doctor in September of 2006. The Neurology Doctor did his usual tests, and nothing medical turned up. Then he did his physical tests. Dee did pretty good with the tests he gave her to do. The Neurology Doctor concluded that Dee had the beginning of Alzheimer's disease. How badly I did not want to hear this. For the first year, I was just supposed to watch her, and its progression. We went back to the Neurology Doctor the next September. Dee had problems doing the tests the doctor gave her. Same report from him, watch her for the next year. All along I could see that things were not getting better. When we went back to the Neurology Doctor in 2008 and Dee tried to do the tests the doctor gave her, she could barely do any part of what he was asking her to do. The Neurology Doctor started Dee on Alzheimer's medication in 2008. He said it might stall the disease for a while. The medication seemed to help her for the first year or two, maybe three, but after that, no change for the better. I have always made sure Dee received the proper medications. The last time we went to see the Neurology Doctor, he said that he wouldn't need to see Dee again unless things changed, but he told me to continue the medications, which I do today. Each morning and night, she gets the medications. Although the Neurology Doctor did not say it, it appeared from his talk that there was no hope of trying to get any thinking process back for Dee. So it has been a steady decline down hill for Dee's memory. Again, I am so sad about this happening to Dee. I often said to myself, why did this have to happen to Dee, such a great person. Dee would never hurt anyone, not animal, person, plant, or anything. And I am saying to everyone, Azheimer's disease is the biggest thief in the world. I hope that someday scientists can find a cure. We donate financially to the Alzheimer's Research Organizations, praying there could someday be a magic pill!

Since 2005, our lives have changed quite a lot. Nothing like I had planned, or even thought about or imagined. Dee has always been my first priority in my life, many times before myself. Her health has always been very important and more so now. I always look and hope for signs of change, any change for the better. I have read much about this Alzheimer's disease. I can see it is a major concern for those who have it. It wrecks the whole person's life. And it makes them dependent on others who care for them. It seems the blood flow through the brain is restricted, and therefore parts of the brain cannot respond to thoughts which regulate reflexes and actions. After a period of time, a person with this disease cannot respond though speech, actions, communications or in any way. But it seems everyone who has been diagnosed with it is affected differently. It is so very sad to see a loved one simply slip away. I knew from the first of our marriage and with what Dee has told me about her upbringing, that she had it tough. It seems there was not much love anywhere in her life, before I met her. Dee did not have a mother. Her father was never around for any support. Her grandmother and grandfather did not have much love to share.

The step-mother hated Dee, and treated her terribly. Her Aunt Pat never wanted Dee, and Dee was only there out of the kindness of Aunt Pat's heart, and pressure from the family. And not a single person from Dee's family has ever tried to get in contact with her. But for me, I am happy for each day that I have with Dee, this Love of My Life. No one ever said life would be perfect, but I am happy for each day, and extremely happy that I am healthy enough to care for Dee's daily needs. I love her so much and I always will.

I am now responsible for all the food preparation, house cleaning, and daily cleansing of Dee. I do have help, to help me with the daily cleansing of Dee, and I also have some help with the house cleaning. I marvel at how our mother prepared all the meals for us growing up, and how she was able to keep our house clean, do the laundry, keep a garden, and help with other outside chores too. Our mother was amazing. In those years, women did not have nearly the amount of modern appliances which we have available today. How did anyone do it? Dee did all these things for me, and us, for all these married years before she was diagnosed. Dee was amazing!! I know I took that all for granted then, but now I realize how difficult these things can be. Dee totally spoiled me!! I wish I had been a better helper for Dee through all the years of our being together. I spend a lot of time reading and searching through all the different cookbooks and recipes that Dee had. I have picked up some recipes myself. I stumble along, but we manage to eat well and be as healthy as we can. My regrets are not being more involved with all the things Dee was doing, before this Alzheimer's disease took control. If there could just be a magic pill to stop Alzheimer's disease, how I pray for that.

In 2006, as Dee's memory loss was increasing, I continually tried my best to help her remember. But there is just no way one person can think, or talk for another person. Alzheimer's disease cannot cover up its destruction of a person. Somewhere I heard that Alzheimer's disease may be partly caused by bad teeth. From all Dee has told me about her early life, especially when she lived with the step mother, Dee did not have proper nutrition. Dee told me, she only had lima beans to eat three times a day for some time. Children certainly need milk and other nutrients from food to develop strong bones and strong teeth. I do not think, from what Dee has told me, that she did have a sufficient supply of milk, or other nutritious foods. That is probably the reason the dentists in New Jersey felt Dee should have her teeth pulled, but would not do so because of her age. Dee did have her upper teeth pulled at some point before we were married, and wore an upper denture plate. Dee then had the bottom teeth pulled around 1970, and a new bottom denture plate put in. Dee has used these same denture plates since that time. I love this woman with her dentures in or out, Dee is my Love.

As I think about the nutrients which Dee did not receive as a child, I think about all the children around the world. So very many of them go hungry each day, and if they find food, it may not have enough nutrients for those children to have a healthy future. In the United States, most of us have a sufficient supply of food. I know Dee told me she had half brothers by the stepmother. I wonder if they had a better upbringing than Dee. I hope they did. I hope the step mother fed them nutritious foods, for normal brain development. Will our people of the world suffer Alzheimer's disease, because of not getting proper foods?

Visiting My Mother

As the years have moved along, Dee and I went to visit my mother every year around Mother's Day. My father died in 1973. Of course we visited most of the family while we were there too. Dee always enjoyed herself, especially visiting with all the kids. The years between 2005 to 2012 were years when we were settling into a comfortable retirement. We went to the casinos several times, and visited some other places that we had already been to. I wanted to see if they were still there, and any changes. We have always enjoyed traveling and seeing all the sights, although traveling out of this country now seems impossible.

On one trip to Indiana, we rode the Amtrak train from Emeryville, Ca. to Chicago, Ill. In Chicago I rented a car to drive to my mother's house in Indiana. It was 2 1/2 days travel time each way on the train, and about a 5 hour drive by auto, from Chicago to my mother's house. I recall how happy Dee was, seeing all the scenery and sights along the train ride, especially in the mountains around Colorado. We got off the train for a few minutes, whenever it stopped for refueling and adding more supplies. We were able to spend a little over an hour at the Denver, Colorado train station. I think I purchased a couple of antique cups and saucers, which had been used as china service for train travel many years in the past. Now, all food is served on throw away articles. We also purchased some food to take along for the rest of the trip. We both enjoyed visiting and talking with many of the other train travelers while on the train. When eating in the dining car, they place you with other travelers, to fill the tables. Dining car space is limited, and most people eat about the same time of day. The dining car could get busy. Dee and I tried to be part of the early group. We always talked with the people sharing our table. Dee loved the trains. She said she used to ride the Pennsylvania trains from New Jersey to Scranton to see her grandmother and then go back to New Jersey while she lived with her Aunt Pat in New Jersey. Because Dee liked the trains so much, I have taken us to many train exhibits and museums and on train rides. We took pictures of most of them, pictures with Dee standing beside and in front of them. I knew she especially liked the steam engines, because they pulled the Pennsylvania trains in the early 50's. Dee and I have been able to ride some steam trains here in California, but only the tourist type rides. I felt the same about trains, because I had a distant relative who worked for the railroad as a maintenance, lubrication person, who worked at a roundhouse. He gave me a ride on a steam engine one time. Fun!! I wish Dee and I could have done that too.

Travel

I truly had planned for us to travel some after we both were retired. Over the years, Dee and I fantasized and dreamed about the different places and countries we would like to see and visit. We even used the globe to search countries, and we had several maps. I had hoped to make those dreams come true. I do travel some now, although mostly only going to the grocery stores, but it is not the same without her. I miss going places with Dee. Without Dee being in the car, driving somehow does not feel quite right. I miss her. But Dee is unable to travel anymore. I always pray for Dee to recover and somehow return to our old ideas and ways. I wish Dee and I could have seen some of those countries we had talked about. I always have hope.

Dee and I have always enjoyed each other's companionship. We never argued. We ate out a lot, talked out our troubles, and made decisions. We talked about going to Europe, and dreamed about other places. Dee and I did travel, but we never went anywhere of any distance. We did drive to visit my aunt and cousin two times, but they only lived a few hours drive away. We also visited my other aunt and cousins, who live in southern California. But all our traveling was here in California, or Nevada, except for going to visit my mother. We really wanted to see other countries, especially in Europe.

Automobiles

Vehicles Dee and I have owned over the 54 years we have been together.

I mentioned the 1959 Impala, which I owned when we met. Then we purchased the 1949 Chevrolet pickup truck in 1968, while we were in Indiana. We sold both the car and truck when we moved back to California. When we arrived back in California, we purchased a 1963 Chevrolet Bel Aire. In 1971, we purchased the 1946 Chevrolet pickup truck. We sold the 1963 Chevrolet in 1979, after we purchased the 1978 Chevrolet Nova. In 1994, we purchased the 1994 Buick. Then in 2009, we purchased the 2009 Chevrolet Cobalt. In 2014, we traded the Chevrolet Cobalt, in on the 2014 Impala, which we currently own. And in 2016, we sold the 1978 Chevrolet Nova.

In November of 1978, Dee was working at Kaiser, and I was steady at Del Monte. This is when we purchased our first new car, a 1978 Chevrolet Nova. What a treat that was. We drove the wheels off it. We would go to San Francisco almost every Sunday after church for our breakfast. Many different places, Cliff House, Mama's, Grovenor's tower, Fairmont hotel, Marina district, Upton's, Lear's greenhouse, Hyatt Regency. and others I'm sure. No place was off limits. We now had air conditioning! We went to Vacaville to the Nut Tree, and Coffee Tree restaurants many many times. We secretly judged where people were from, while we were sitting outside, and waiting to be seated. And we would guess at what type of work they did, (which of course we never knew) but only for our fun of it. Dee and I just loved having fun. We traveled well together, and had tons of fun. I miss that terribly. Dee is, and was, great!

We ate at many places if they were good, and never went back if the food was not good. We went to every place. We had fun together. On some days we would leave the house at 6:30 am, and not get back until 5 pm. We would drive to Stockton, just to eat breakfast, or dinner. One time we took Jim Riley with us, he said we were crazy to drive that far just to eat (65 miles). We also went to San Juan Batista, about 75 miles, to the Flying Lady in Gilroy, California. We investigated many places, and loved doing this.

 The 1978 Chevy Nova. It had 206,000 miles when I sold it. We had purchased a new 1994 Buick, in January, 1994. It had 156,000 miles on it when it was stolen in 2007. I had also driven it a lot. Then I continued driving the '78 Nova. We had a new 2009 Chevrolet Cobalt with 53,000 miles on it when we traded it in on our current 2014 Impala. I drove it a lot. Dee and I loved to be together and travel, even though we never went very far. I bought this Impala because Dee had so much trouble getting in cars. The Impala has the largest space between the seat and door frame to enter or exit. This is why I purchased it. Dee could get into this Impala by herself if she wanted to, there is plenty of space. Dee has not been able to ride in our old truck for probably 20 years. But she loved it years ago, when she did ride in it. Now I do drive very little and usually only for shopping. There is nowhere I really want to go by myself.

 In 1994 we had purchased the new Buick Century automobile. At that time, the old Chevy had almost 160,000 miles on it, so I felt we needed something to give it some deserved help and rest. We did not sell the Chevy because I continued driving it to work. We also drove the Buick a lot, as we were still traveling all around northern California. And we also drove it to see my Aunt and cousins who lived in the San Diego area, plus another Aunt and cousin in northern California.

 We probably drove the Buick to Disneyland, not sure, but I know we drove the Chevy to Disneyland two times. A few years prior to driving to Disneyland, we had taken a bus tour to Disneyland. The time was limited with the bus trip. Then we decided to make the drive there, as we could spend as much time as we wanted. On these trips, we would stay at a nearby hotel. It was not as expensive at that time. We would usually go into Disneyland Park for two days. We shopped, and rode most of the rides. And always ate at their restaurants. Several of the employees there have a wonderful sense of humor! And their dancing was fabulous! We really became kids there, both of us, and we enjoyed it so much.

And down the street from Disneyland in Garden Grove, California, is a wonderful restaurant. It served the most delicious strawberry pies. We also ate there, the food was average, but the pies were excellent. We wanted to bring a couple strawberry pies home with us, but they would have spoiled. They needed to be refrigerated. As I have said before, we were always searching for good places to eat, and to recommend to other friends traveling to Disneyland. This was one.

Even though I tried my best to maintain our vehicles as best I could, everything wears out. The Buick had taken Dee and me on many casino trips, and to Reno too. Then one morning in September 2007 I got up and walked out to our driveway. The Buick was not there. At first I thought I had left it in the shop somewhere. But I kept thinking, "No, I had not left it anywhere," as I had driven it the day before. I talked to Dee about this situation, because I usually told Dee of my plans for having auto repairs taken care of. Someone had stolen it! It was gone! I called the police and reported it stolen about 8am. The police took the report, and said they would look for it. Later that evening, about 10pm, the police called and said they had found the car. They wanted me to come and drive it home. The Buick was in East Oakland. I would not go to that area by myself, especially after dark. That meant Dee had to go with me. I called a taxi to take us there. The police department said the officer would wait for us there. When we arrived, the car had been stripped, and was not drive-able. The policeman was there, but because the car was not drive-able, I had to call the tow truck to pick it up. That meant Dee and I would have to wait on the sidewalk until the tow truck arrived. It was a good hour before the tow truck came. In the meantime the policeman did not want to leave us, two white people in a black neighborhood at 11pm that night. The policeman stayed as long as he could, but did get a call, and had to leave. He came back after a few minutes, about the same time as the tow truck arrived. Until the tow truck came, Dee and I had to wait, and stand on the sidewalk. The tow truck driver loaded the car on the truck, and we brought it back to our house and put it in our driveway. I called the insurance company the next day. The insurance adjuster came, looked at it and declared it a total loss. I told the insurance company I no longer wanted it. They paid us the value of the car and took it away. We still had the old Chevy. Then I had some upgrades done to the Chevy, to make it look better, and more comfortable. We drove the Chevy for the next year. Then in November of 2008, we purchased a 2009 Chevrolet Cobalt. I always wanted something more comfortable than the old Chevy for Dee to ride in. Dee had a hard time getting in and out of the old Chevy, as her walking had declined. She was able to get into the Cobalt much more easily. Now, as more things have happened and changed for Dee, we use the Impala.

Most of our traveling now is to the medical doctors. I have to say, the Impala is a nice car to drive. We do have a prior relationship with Impalas because I had purchased a 1959 Impala in 1962. It was the car I was driving when I met Dee. Dee liked it, and it took me across this county four times, from Indiana to California twice and back. Dee was always my partner as I traveled. We traveled well together. I love her.

Visitors

Many things have happened over the recent years, since Dee has had Alzheimer's disease. Karma, Gayle's daughter, has come to visit from southern California many times. It is always great to see and catch up with her on visits. She and her husband usually share a meal with us. Sometimes we have met at a restaurant and sometimes I have fixed something here at our house. Dee was so happy to see Karma. Karma had known Dee for sometime before Dee and I met. Dee used to babysit them. All Gayle's daughters have been so wonderful to Dee. They really loved Dee from the time they were little. They have told me a few things they learned from Dee, while Dee watched them. I guess Dee was pretty strict!!

My sister and brother-in-law came to visit us from Indiana. They usually stay at a hotel, as our house is pretty small. We always had fun taking them around to the sights. When we were able to attend a show in San Francisco, that was a highlight for all of us too. My sister is not interested in sports, so we did not attend any ball games. It is always a beautiful thing to show people around the sights. Taking guests to see and walk on the Golden Gate Bridge is popular. If anyone comes to visit, the bridge is usually one of the main sights to visit. There are many other sights to see around this area. The bridge is always first and then other sites which do not have so much fame or notoriety; there is plenty to see and occupy our time while visiting. The Oakland Bay Bridge is an exceptional site to see and mention too.

My brother and sister-in-law came a few years ago. But they only stayed for a day or two. I do not recall being able to take them to see any of the usual, great sights. And I do not recall the year they were here. But the whole family had all been here once before in 1980. I believe we showed them most of the highlights at that time. Seems like it could not have been so long ago, but that was the year. In 1980 they had all driven here in my brother's van. My brother, sister, sister-in-law, their 2 kids, and my mother. I heard they had quite an experience!!

Many years ago, our friends from Arkansas stopped for a visit. They were only here for a very few hours. At that time, they were long haul truck drivers. They had their load, delivered it here, and then had a backhaul, and needed to deliver that load at a certain time. But it was wonderful to see them, even though it was a short visit. We keep in contact with them by telephone, and cards. Wonderful people!

My Mother's Health

Later in the year 2012, my mother's health began failing, faster than I had thought at the time. Dee and I had visited Indiana in the middle of that year. As my mother was getting worse, I visited her again in September for a week and planned to visit again within the next ten days. Of course, I kept in touch with frequent phone calls with my sister, and brother-in-law. My mother was living with my sister at that time. My mother needed to go to the doctors and was truly not able to care for herself at all. My sister and brother-in-law did the best they could to care for her, it's just that her body was wearing out. Her doctors had placed her in a nursing home on two different occasions but she had not done well there and wanted to live with my sister and brother-in-law. My sister moved my mother from the nursing home, back to her house. My mother had known she had a leaky Mitral valve in her heart for a very long time, but always opted to do nothing about it, except medication. My mother always believed in the local doctors, and thought they were the best. That really was not true, but she refused to go to specialists, or anyone she thought would change any treatments she might have already been treated with. A few years before she died, she had treatment that really required specialized doctors, but she refused any other help. I tried to convince her to consult a specialist. No, she would not. She would have been better off if she had. I feel the last few years of her life would have been much easier and less painful. It appeared to me that both my mother and father thought all doctors were magicians and could make everything well.

My mother died October 4, 2012. Dee had stayed here in Oakland, when I went back to Indiana in September, and Carol stayed with Dee. Carol has been a very good friend to Dee and myself for all these years. Carol met Dee when they both worked at Kaiser. But when my mother died, Dee of course traveled to Indiana with me to the funeral. Carol stayed at our house here to care for our cats, mail, etc. while we were gone. Dee and I stayed with my sister at that time, for about a week or a little more, I do not remember how long. But while we were there, after we had attended my mother's funeral, we three heirs met with Susan, our mother's attorney who was handling my mother's estate's legal matters. The six of us were present, myself, my sister and my brother and our spouses, to ensure that all parties knew exactly how mom had wanted her estate to be divided. After reading her will, we all three knew our mother's desires. My inheritance share was the inheritance of a 160 acre property but I needed to add some of our saved money to make this acquisition complete.

In June of 2013, I became responsible for that property. I had to pay the taxes, maintenance, and any other things of importance. And as for the farmer who rented it, we renewed the contract. Then in late October, Dee and I went back to Indiana again to work on the property. It needed a lot of care, as it had been neglected for many years. Dee and I were there for about 5 weeks if I remember correctly. My sister cared for Dee, while her husband and I worked on the farm issues. We did a lot of things and made lots of progress. Some days were bitter cold, and it snowed too. My sister brought Dee over to the farm to see what we were doing on a couple occasions. That was so nice. We had a fire going to burn trash, and my sister wanted to have a hot dog roast. That would have been great, but the weather was too cold and nasty. My sister is the greatest, and she took really good care of Dee. It was not easy for my sister, but Dee was in a little better physical condition then. Dee was able to stand and walk, even though her memory was bad. Now, Dee's and my estate includes this property. Although Dee's memory is not so great, she would have wanted me to care for the property that my father and mother had worked so hard to maintain and to make it a more successful piece of land.

In October of 2014, Dee and I again went to Indiana. This time we worked on the farm again. We cleared more of the overgrowth and I hired some help. I also hired a contractor to fix some problems. It was not so cold this time. Again, my sister watched Dee. One day we all went to Columbus, Indiana to visit one of my schoolmates for lunch, mainly because my sister said she liked to do some day trips, to get away from working all the time, and we did work all the time. But day trips are fun too. We definitely needed a break. And whenever Dee and I were in Indiana, we always visited the rest of my family too. Sadly, that schoolmate has passed since our visit.

For Dee and I to travel, I would put her in a wheelchair, so we could travel through the airports a little faster. We had our own wheelchair which went with us. Dee could never have walked from one gate to another for the changing of flights. At that time Dee could walk, but very slowly. I also requested for us to board our plane early, as it took extra time for me to walk Dee to her seat. All went pretty smoothly. The biggest problem was taking Dee to the bathroom on the airplanes. Some planes have a curtain to pull around the bathroom door, which gives more privacy and space. But the bathrooms are small, only large enough for one person. The airports usually have a family bathroom, so we would use the family bathroom about 30 minutes before time for us to get on the plane. I also watched what we consumed at the airports.

Another crazy thing about our lives many years ago, Dee and I would go mostly to the Oakland airport, in the evenings, to eat our dinner, and to just sit and watch the people walk by. We would also stand and look at the planes coming in and taking off. We also went to the Nut Tree in Vacaville, California, to watch the small planes come in. Vacaville has a small airport. The people would get out of their planes and go into the restaurant to eat. We would look at the different planes, and think about what we could do if we had one. They would only seat about 4 people. A lot of the planes were for sale. We were dreamers!! We thought traveling this way would be fun!

In 2015, I went to Indiana again. Carol stayed and cared for Dee here at our home and cared for the kitties, the garden, etc. again. Carol is a good person and she took good care of Dee. I do not remember all that I did in Indiana on the farm, but we worked on different things. I know I had Lawson fix the ditch in 2014 and in 2015 I had Tom bury a bunch of trash in the corner of the woods, trash that had accumulated by others putting it there. That was not the proper place for that kind of trash. My brother-in-law and I were able to dispose of a bunch of tires first, and then the rest of the trash was buried. On that trip, I hired Cory to help me cut down the overgrown fence rows and dispose of the remains. There was a problem with a ditch in the other field and I asked Tom to fix it, along with a wash that had started causing severe soil erosion. Tom also buried some rocks that had been thrown in the corner of that field, along with burying some very hazardous thorn trees. So far the clean up has gone well and has done good for the property. After our father died in 1973, that property had not had much care and attention, if any. There had been much neglect. My mother did not know how the scale of neglect had grown and accumulated after my father died.

In 2016, I made plans to go to Indiana to work on the farm again. My sister also has property and I planned to help her while I was there. I made arrangements for Dee to stay at an assisted living facility. I had checked it out before, talked extensively with the manager and thought it was the kind of place that treated people very well. It had been recommended to me by a qualified agency. I took Dee there with her belongings, from November 1st, to November 15th, for 15 days. Because of Dee's poor memory, she had to be placed and cared for on the Memory Care Floor. Dee adapted pretty well, she seemed to like it. They fed her, bathed her, and she attended their classes. I did check on Dee the morning I was leaving to catch my plane for Indiana. I found Dee walking in the hallway with her walker. She had dirtied her pants sometime before I arrived. I wondered how long it could have been, before someone checked on her, to see if she needed to be changed. But I took her to her room, cleaned her in the shower, and put clean clothes on her. I then took her over to the activity room, where she sat in with some of the other residents. This is where the staff entertain the residents. Then I left and proceeded to catch the plane for my trip. While I was away, I called every day to talk to The Med Tech, to ask how Dee was doing. I was told by the staff there to ask for the Med Tech if I wanted to check on Dee, to ask how she was doing. The reply I was always given was, "Dee is doing good". I was convinced that in the future this would be a good place for Dee to stay. I also thought this would be a good facility for Dee to be placed, if and when it became the necessary time for others to care for Dee permanently. I liked this place. But of course, I would always take as good of care of Dee, as I could, here at home with me. When I picked Dee up on the 15th, everything seemed OK. The staff there seemed to have been happy to have Dee to care for. The staff said to me as we were leaving, to bring

Dee back anytime. They said, "We will be happy to care for Dee". After we returned home, Dee and I settled in for the remainder of the year. We celebrated the holidays, and had happy times for the rest of that year.

During the year of 2017, I took Dee to this same assisted living facility a few times. Always on Sundays, because they have entertainment to entertain the residents living there. They sent brochures to our home inviting us and telling us about the entertainment scheduled for the month. I felt it was good to try to attend, to support the workers there, and the morale of all involved. Their entertainment was mostly local musical people, and most were very good. We enjoyed this. It was only for a couple hours, but it appeared most everyone was pleased and happy, and enjoying the afternoon. Dee and I enjoyed the music, and our Sunday afternoons with their entertainment. But by then, Dee had begun a big decrease in her speaking ability. Dee could say Yes, and No, but not much of anything else.

My Trip to See Dee's Childhood Home

During the early part of 2017, I used Ancestry.com., to see what I could discover about Dee's childhood home, and Scranton, Pennsylvania. I used Google Earth to try to find the Scranton Pennsylvania Catholic Cemetery, where Dee's mother and Dee's grandmother Hennigan are buried. I did not know before this that both Dee's mother Mary, and Dee's grandmother Mary Hennigan were both buried in the same cemetery. Ancestry.com gave me the dates, and I did not know they were buried side by side. Dee's grandfather Hennigan died in 1927, and is buried somewhere around Chicago. I found the burial plots for Dee's grandmother and Dee's mother. I also learned that Dee's father is buried in Quantico, Virginia, beside the stepmother. Dee's father died in1991. On

Ancestry.com. I also found the area where Dee lived as a child, the rooming house, Holy Rosary Church, and the school. I was able to get the address and a picture of Dee's grandparents' (Hennigan's) house. In my mind, I thought that if I found these places, and took some pictures of them, it could possibly arouse some memories in Dee. It seemed to me to be the only and the last thing I could do to try to help Dee's memory. I hoped it would have a positive effect.

My sister lives in Indiana. I talked to my sister about the idea of going to Pennsylvania, and because her and her husband like to travel, I asked if they would be interested in making this trip with me. They both said yes, and also said that we could travel in their Chevrolet pickup truck, as it has lots of room. A big benefit, the three of us would get to see some scenery which we had never seen before. I thought the whole idea was a positive thing. I wanted to do this for Dee. Even though Dee never wanted to travel there in our earlier years, I somehow thought it would be good to have some pictures to show to Dee.

I picked out the dates, coordinated them with my sister, and made all the hotel reservations and arrangements. I also chose a couple things to do and see along the way, as this would probably be a one time only trip. I doubted if I would ever have a chance to travel to this area again. I wanted to see an old Navy buddy's family, who live in upstate New York and anything else of interest we may see, before reaching Scranton, Pennsylvania. For this trip, I had made previous arrangements for Dee to stay at the same assisted living facility, where she had stayed the previous year, in 2016. Dee did well then, and I had confidence they would take good care of her. The same management people were there, and made all the arrangements with me. They assured me they would take good care of Dee. I truly trusted them. I felt Dee would have good care.

To make this trip, I took Dee to the same assisted living facility, just like I did the year before. I took Dee there on Monday,

October 23, 2017, during the afternoon. I was going to fly to Indianapolis airport on Tuesday, October 24, 2017. My flight departed Oakland at 6am, so I had no time to check on Dee the morning before I left. My sister and brother in law picked me up at the Indianapolis airport. We stopped on the way to my sister's house to eat at a Country Kitchen restaurant then we went back to their house and rested that evening. I called the assisted living facility that evening, to ask about Dee and was told she was doing fine.

The next day, my sister and I looked over the properties we own, and talked about upgrades we would like to do to improve them. We also lined up our supplies for our trip to Scranton, the following day. I had planned for this to be a six day trip, before we would get back to my sister's home, in Indiana. Again that evening I called the assisted living facility, and checked on Dee: "She is doing well," I was told.

The next morning, Thursday, October 26, 2017, we started off. We drove across Ohio, and stopped at the Football Hall of Fame Museum, in Canton, Ohio. We ate at different places along the way. We drove along parts of Lake Erie, and stayed our first night in Erie, Pennsylvania. I again called the assisted living facility and asked for the Med Tech to check to see how Dee was doing, but they did not answer. I realized the time difference between the two states, it was probably eating time at the assisted living facility. They were probably too busy to answer the phone. I have no idea where the telephones were located for the staff.

The next morning, October 27, 2017, after eating breakfast at our hotel, we drove on towards our destination of Rome, New York. I had decided to see my Navy buddy's family, before going on to Scranton. We stopped at a Panera restaurant for our lunch. I am not sure if it was in Pennsylvania, or New York State. This was Friday, October 27th. We had ordered our food. This was about 12:30pm, Ohio time. While at the restaurant, I received a call from the assisted living facility where Dee was staying. I was told that Dee had been taken to Kaiser ER, because Dee's forehead was bleeding. Dee has a mole/wart on her forehead, and sometimes she scratches it and it will bleed some. It usually is hidden by her hair and not easily seen.. That is what I thought had happened, and that is what did happen, she had scratched it. Kaiser ER treated it, applied some first aid ointment along with a band aid covering, and sent Dee back to the assisted living facility. Bleeding from the wart/mole on Dee's forehead is something that happens every once in a while, but it usually needs to be scratched first. This bleeding happens occasionally, but it is never serious. Dee must have been nervous and scratched it enough to make it bleed. This was not an emergency, but of course the staff at the assisted living facility would not have known that. And I had never mentioned it to them before, as this may happen only once in a couple years. When I was filling out the paperwork for Dee's staying there, I just did not remember this. If they had called me at the time, I could have told them to just wash the blood off, and apply a little first aid ointment. Afterwards, I wished I had put that information down on the paperwork. But I just forgot to mention this wart/mole to the employees at the assisted living facility, when I filled out their paperwork.

After our food came at Panera, and before I was finished eating, I received another call from the assisted living facility. I believe it was a different person who called this time. They explained to me that Dee had developed a blister on her left foot. Because Dee wears a brace on that foot, I imagined someone had put her brace on incorrectly, and created a blister on the side of her leg, ankle, or that area. But they told me that they would have their nurse treat it, and put a bandage on it. No one ever explained that this was a huge blister on Dee's heel. At that discussion I felt relief, thinking it would get treatment right away, and I did not think it was important enough for me to cancel the rest of my trip. Yes, I was worried, but here I was on our trip. I thought about the situation, but I had confidence in management at the assisted living facility, to handle this situation. I was convinced they would take good care of Dee, and treat any injuries correctly. I decided Dee would be OK. Then we left the Panera restaurant, and drove on to Rome, New York. At our arrival, we found our hotel, checked in for our three night stay, found something to eat, and settled in for the night. Again, I called the assisted living facility that night to check on Dee, and was told, "She is doing fine." There was no mention about any blister, at that call. I felt relieved and thought Dee would be OK. I see now, that my mistake was not calling the manager, whom I had made all the arrangements with, to ask that person about Dee's condition. I prayed for Dee.

New York State

For our visit to my Navy friend Jim's family. I had made arrangements with Jim's granddaughter to meet with her the next morning, Saturday. Our arrival was going to be a surprise, because the granddaughter wanted to keep it a secret. That was okay by me. I knew Jim had died in 2009, but I had always wanted to get up to visit with him. Even though Jim was not there, I still wanted to meet with and visit his family. Jim was my good Navy friend and I never wanted to lose contact with him. When Jim was still alive, he and I talked over the phone once or twice a year, we exchanged cards and usually talked around Christmas time too. I had tried to get to see Jim many times over the years, but never was able to make the visit for one reason or another before he died. But I still wanted to meet his family. I felt somewhat close to them through Jim, even though he was deceased. And as I have said, this would probably be my only opportunity to visit them and his gravesite.

Jim and I had become pretty good friends while we were in the Navy Seabees together, especially while we were in Viet-Nam. We were of the same rank, Steelworker. One of the things he did for me, and which I will never, never forget!! I had a bad case of flash burn from welding that day, due to the overcast, cloudy weather. Flashburn feels like someone has put a handful of sand in your eyes. That night Jim could see that I was in big trouble. I could not open my eyes, I could not see anything. Then Jim walked me, hand in hand, across the camp to the Medical Corpsman. The Corpsman put drops in my eyes, and then I could see again. Oh what a relief that was, a miracle for me. I could not see anything before. Again, I will never forget what Jim did for me that evening, and how much I appreciated his caring for his fellow Seabee. Jim and I were sharing the same living area, which consisted of a poncho tied between two trees, over the sand. We each had our own cots for sleeping. The sand was everywhere but we learned to live with it. We ate sea rations out of cans for quite a long time, that was our food supply. After working hard all the time, a person can eat most anything. Many people complained about the food, but the rations kept us going. After a few months, the dining hall had been constructed and supplied and was open to feed all of us. Somewhere, the Battalion had found clean drinking water, and stored it in a tank trailer, so now we had clean drinking water. We bathed in the ocean. And where do you put the soap when you bathe in the ocean??? Down on the ocean floor!! Then it becomes sandpaper. Jim and I worked together, trained together, played together, drank together, and whatever else we did. We worked hard. Jim and I both had strong backs, so we were a team while building the airstrip out of aluminum matting for airplanes to land and take off on. Because we were doing a good job, we were chosen to keep doing this until the airstrip was completed. The panels were heavy. The heat/air was hot as all get out all the time, even at night. The sun usually shone bright all day. But when the Monsoon rain season came, huge rains came hard and kept coming. I don't know how the sky can hold so much water. We were the first Seabee Battalion to arrive in VietNam in May, 1965. We survived!

On Saturday, October 28, 2017, we drove about 30 miles to Jim's daughter's house. The granddaughter was sitting, and waiting on the porch for us. The whole family was so surprised to see us. We visited for a while, and then the daughter and granddaughter took us to see Jim's grave site, and other places Jim's family lived before living at their current address. We went to lunch at a restaurant in Boonville, NewYork and met more of Jim's relatives, even his youngest. Then we went to meet Jim's wife, and the rest of Jim's children, and his in-laws and some more grandchildren. Jim and his wife had 7 children. It was so good to see where Jim lived before he died, and especially his family. Jim had told me about the farm where they all lived. Jim's granddaughter had a horse. Another daughter milked cows all the time, for her neighbor. We were shown all the beautiful countryside. We met the granddaughter's horse. We met the sister at the farm where she milked, and saw the dairy cows too. We also met the granddaughter's brother, and another grandson of Jim's. Late in the afternoon, early evening, we went back to our hotel for the night. We picked up food, nearby the hotel, and ate in our rooms. I again called the assisted living facility, and checked on Dee. I do not remember if I talked to anyone there or not.

Then on Sunday, we met and went to see a horse equipment show, with the granddaughter, and her mother (Jim's daughter), and father. On Sunday evening, October 29, 2017, we all met at a nice restaurant that the sister had chosen. The food was great, Jim's family were all there, and there were lots of laughs. There were about 30 people in our group. What fun it was visiting with all of them. It was really great for me to see all of Jim's family, and the surrounding area. Beautiful people, and beautiful countryside. I have very fond memories of that remarkable dinner that evening, and all our visiting with Jim's family. After our dinner, everyone went their own way, and the three of us went back to our hotel. We settled in our rooms, and I again called the assisted living facility, to ask how Dee was doing. I was told Dee is doing fine.

After our three night stay, and visiting with Jim's family, we departed Rome, New York. This was the morning of Monday, October 30, 2017. We started driving toward Scranton, Pennsylvania. On our way, we stopped in Cooperstown, New York, to see the Baseball Hall of Fame Museum. We spent some time at the museum, looking at all the baseball history. We ate our lunch in Cooperstown, New York, at one of the recommended eateries. That restaurant serves a burger shaped like a baseball. It looked like a baseball, tasted good, and was a treat. We then continued our drive toward Scranton, Pennsylvania.

Scranton, Pennsylvania

It was late Monday evening when we arrived in Scranton, Pennsylvania. We found our hotel, checked in, and went to a nearby restaurant to eat. Scranton is a bigger city than I thought it was. After eating, we went back to the hotel, and to our rooms. I again called the assisted living facility to check on Dee, and was told Dee was doing good. I usually tried to call around 7pm, or later, California time, but before 8pm.

The next morning, in Scranton, Tuesday October 31, 2017, we ventured out to find the cemetery, the church, and school, and Dee's house where she lived as a young child. We located the cemetery, drove in, and started looking for Dee's mothers grave. I had the plot number, but having no knowledge of the area, I had to ask where to look. Because Dee's mother was buried in 1945, I thought it would be in the older section. There were a few monuments, but no marker for most graves. There are some trees there, slightly hilly, but all grass. Only a few headstones. I could not see anything, marking Dee's mother's grave. I went into the office, and asked if someone could help me find these grave sites. The director looked up the plot numbers, and found where he thought they would be, and came out to the area with me. Luckily, he had taken the layout book with him. He could not find the sites at first, but after a while he showed me the location. There were no markers for Mary Pallard or Dee's grandmother Hennigan. The two are buried beside each other, Dee's biological mother, and Dee's Hennigan grandmother. I did not know they were buried side by side. Mary Pallard died in 1945, and Mary Hennigan (grandmother) died in 1961. Back in the office, they told me that John Hennigan had purchased these plots. It could have been John Pallard who purchased these plots, but the office told me it was John Hennigan. It probably was John Pallard who purchased these plots, and the cemetery has the wrong name for the purchaser. I have no idea when John Hennigan could have purchased these plots, because he died in 1927. That is when Dee's mother saw her father get killed by a train at the train switchyard. Maybe Mary Hennigan purchased them using John Hennigan's name in 1945, a possibility. John Hennigan is buried around Chicago, where he was originally from, according to Ancestry.com.. The Hennigan's had two daughters, Mary was the youngest. Somehow, there was a $400 bill still owed on these plots. I paid the $400, to clear the debt, and was told there would never be any more charges for these sites. If Dee had been with me, she would have done the same thing. At the entrance to the cemetery is a monument company. As we were leaving, I went in and ordered a monument to mark their graves. Because they are buried side by side, one marker with both names and dates on it would serve the purpose. The company agreed to make the marker, take it over to the cemetery and the cemetery personnel would then place it on the correct graves. I have no idea if anyone will ever look for these graves. A couple weeks later, I received a photo showing the marker on the gravesites.

Dee's grandmother Palaskas is buried somewhere in New Jersey. Dee's grandfather Palaskas is buried in Nicholson, Pennsylvania. And as I have mentioned, Dee's father is buried in Quantico, Virginia. Dee always told me John was a United States government employee. I understand this cemetery is for deceased FBI and other government employees.

We left the cemetery area and drove through Scranton, but not through downtown. We found the street of the Palaskas residence, Dee's childhood home, the church, and the school. The house was some kind of rooming house at one time, because the windows on the second floor are very small, and there are several of them. Dee said that is where the mine workers roomed, before her grandparents moved in. Dee said the rooms were small. In front of this house was Noon's grocery store. This is the store Dee's father worked and managed when Dee was little. The grocery store is still there, with the same name. Next to the store was the alley. And next to that was the creek/ditch where Dee was forbidden to go, but she did anyway. She liked playing there. I could only see a small trickle of water at the bottom. A short distance from the house and grocery store was the church. It was called the Holy Rosary when Dee lived there but has a different name now. The church was locked. It looked like it had remained a Catholic church. The school is next to the church, and it appeared to have been closed also. Next to the school was a building that must have been the Rectory. The church, school, and rectory, were all made of the same materials, and looked all the same. At one time, this must have been a large Catholic community. There was no one around to answer any of the questions I had. There were no children around and it appeared the school was closed. I would have loved to see the inside of the church. It looked like it must have been a nice, working class, mostly Lithuanian neighborhood at the time Dee lived there. This probably would have been the late 30's, and around the start of WWII. Dee never told me if her father and his brother and sisters lived there when they were born. I would think they did. John was the oldest of the children, and he was born in 1911. And Marion, John's sister, was the youngest and she lived in this same house when Dee was a little girl.

After looking around for a while, we left the house and church area and found the Hennigan grandparent's house. It was quite some distance away, but Dee told me she used to walk there, and walked it many times. For a little girl, it seemed to be a long way to walk. But Dee was a determined little kid, I am sure! The Hennigan grandparents begged John to let them raise Dee, after their daughter's death, (Dee's mother). And Dee really liked them. Of course, Dee liked her grandmother, Marcella too. But John said no. There must have been hard feelings between the Hennigan family and John Pallard.

Dee's mother died in a mental hospital in 1945. She died from tuberculosis. This disease was a bad virus around that time. According to the doctors who treated Mary, they felt that if Mary had children, it could trigger a difficult time for her mentally. The reason was, because of Mary seeing her father getting killed by the train, at the railroad yard, when she was only 9 years old. According to Dee, John had promised the Hennigan family, Mary would not get pregnant! But Dee is the child of that situation, which probably resulted in Mary's breakdown. Mary Pallard was confined to the mental hospital when Dee was only one year old. Dee's grandmother Marcella Palaskas, Marion Palaskas, and John then cared for Dee. And because Mary was in the County mental hospital, John would never take Dee to see her real, (biological) mother at that hospital. Dee never saw her real mother, Mary, alive. Dee was able to see her mother, when she was in her coffin at the funeral home, after Mary had died, and was to be buried. Dee asked her father, who was that, and

John told Dee, it was her mother. Dee said Mary was a very petite lady, lots of red hair, laying in her coffin. And Dee's mother Mary had on a pretty pink dress. Dee precisely remembered the pink dress, and how pretty it was. That is all Dee could remember about her real, biological mother. What a sad story, I felt so sad for Dee, when she told me this. Such a sad, sad story. But Dee has always been tough, and handled things in her own way. Dee never showed much, if any emotions, about her family.

I took as many pictures of the things as I could of these areas of Scranton, Pennsylvania, while we were there. The cemetery, the church, Dee's house, the grandparents house, the creek, etc.. I brought them back and showed them to Dee, hoping they would stir something. Dee looked at them. Oh how I had wished they would excite Dee, but she showed no reaction at all. But I was happy to get to see all of this. But it did not prove to be of any help to Dee, the Alzheimer's had already taken its terrible toll. It seems to me, from what Dee has told me over the years, Dee must not have had many happy memories of Scranton, and all she experienced there. But I do know Dee told me she used to ride the train from New Jersey, to Scranton, to see her grandmothers. It was never clear whom Dee went to visit, but I know she did not care for Newark, New Jersey. But Dee liked riding the steam trains.

This was a rewarding experience for me, to be able to see where Dee lived. And the area where Dee was born, and lived as a little girl. I did not look for the condemned house, which Dee had told me so much about. It probably had been torn down. That is where Dee was made to live with her step mother, and I am sure there were no happy memories from there. But Dee said it was close to the church and school. And while Dee lived with the stepmother in the condemned house, Dee had to walk past Noon's grocery to get to school, and then back to the condemned house. And the grandmother's house was just behind Noon's grocery. The stepmother had forbidden Dee from stopping to see her grandmother Marcella anytime. That must have been so difficult, the deep fear the step mother had put into Dee. That step mother could not have been a very nice person.

As I have mentioned before, to make this trip I placed Dee in the same assisted living facility as I had done in 2016. I had taken Dee and her belongings there on Oct. 23, 2017. I left town the following day. I thought the assisted living facility was a very nice place, and I was assured they would take excellent care of Dee. I called every day to inquire about how Dee was doing. Again, I had liked the place and had a good experience with it in 2016. The assisted living facility called me on October 27th, 2017, and told me of Dee being taken to Kaiser ER for the bleeding on the side of her head. Kaiser treated it, and sent her back to the assisted living facility. Then a short time later they called again, and told me Dee had developed a blister on her left foot. This is the situation I mentioned earlier. I asked about the seriousness of the situation, but they told me they were going to have their nurse look at it and treat it. I later found that they had no nurse on the staff, and 10 days passed before they did get a nurse to look at the wound. I felt confident the staff would take good care of the situation. I was assured by management, they would take good care of any issues that could arise. I trusted them. And as a check, I called every day, usually in the evening to talk to the Med Tech, and to inquire about Dee and her care. Every time I called, and was able to talk to someone, the person always told me Dee was doing just fine. Most of the time they told me she was in the activities room. I had experienced their schedule from the year before, so I sort of knew the activities going on there. Mostly, it was a well thought out facility. As I have said, I called every day. Later, I was shocked about the care this facility had taken of Dee.

After completing our travels to New York, and Scranton, Pennsylvania, we returned back to Indiana. We returned to Indiana on Wednesday, November 1, 2017. There I spent the next few days working on our properties. We were able to get many things accomplished, and were able to get contractors to take care of some other things which needed to be taken care of. I was able to visit many of my relatives too. On November 14th, 2017, my sister and brother-in-law took me back to Indianapolis. I stayed in a hotel in Indianapolis that night, because the hotel furnished transportation the next morning back to the airport. My flight departed Thursday morning, at 8 am.

My Returning to California

I arrived home here in Oakland on the afternoon of Nov. 15, 2017, and after I put my things away, I got in my car and went to pick up Dee at the assisted living facility. Luckily I was able to park in their garage, close to the entrance door. I went in, signed in, and went up to Dee's room. Dee was not there. Then I went to the activities room to get Dee to bring her home, because of the time of day I thought I would find her there. This was about 5pm, maybe a little later, I do not remember looking at my watch. The residents had already had their evening meal, when I arrived at the activity room. I saw one employee, and about a dozen residents there. They were watching TV, but I did not see Dee. I kept looking. Sitting in a wheelchair, feet dragging, slumped over, head down was another person. I picked up the head, which was unconscious, and saw my Dee! But I did not recognize her at first. I was mystified. How could this be my Dee? Sadly, it was! I thought, Oh my goodness, what have they done to my Dee? Then I pushed her back to her room in the wheelchair she was in, and I was able to manhandle her onto the toilet. I wiped her face, and she became a little responsive, but very little. Dee was dead weight. I was able to get her clothes off. Then I washed her face, as it had dirt on it. Then I put clean clothes on her, but she could not stand up, as she was very out of it! But I was able to get her back into the wheelchair. Then I placed all Dee's clothing in the boxes I had used for this occasion. The room had clothes all over the floor, some dirty, and all her toiletries were locked in the cabinet. I knew I needed to get Dee out of this place. Then I found a male employee to come and help me, to get us both, Dee and me, and her belongings, down to and into our car. This was very difficult to do. Dee was unconscious. There was no discussion between the employee who helped me, and myself.

I knew that Dee's condition was critical, if she was going to survive this situation. I was afraid Dee would not survive it. I had never seen anyone in a rundown condition like that! I drove straight to Kaiser Emergency Room, and asked the doctor there to help me get my Dee out of the car, and into the ER room. A male doctor, and 3 lady nurses went to the car, and managed to get Dee into a wheelchair. They took her in, and put her into bed, and proceeded to examine Dee. By this time, Dee was a little awake, but very sleepy. She was severely dehydrated, had not eaten for some time, and had this huge blister on her left foot heel. The doctor kept Dee in the ER for a few hours, and then told me they were going to admit her. OK, I said. There was no other decision which could be made. The ER doctor was very upset at seeing Dee's condition. He asked me what had happened. They suspected I had neglected Dee while caring for her here at home, and that had caused all these problems. I said, "OH NO!" I had gone away for 3 weeks, and had put Dee in an assisted living memory care facility, to care for her while I went to check on this other business. And I called there to check on Dee each day. I was always given the response, "Dee is doing great, or doing very well". This doctor was extremely upset at Dee's condition, and asked me the name of the place. I told him, and that was the end of that. But I did find out later, Kaiser made a complaint to the state authorities, about this mistreatment. And the State fined the assisted living facility, on Dee's account, because of their poor care. I feel Dee would probably have died in that place if I had not come to pick her up when I did. After another day, she may not have made it. I was very disappointed, and upset to see her in this condition. I kept asking myself, how could anyone neglect Dee, and allow her to get to this terrible condition? I had trusted the assisted living facility. I assume they just did not want to be bothered with her, and Dee was probably stubborn, because she was probably scared!!

The ER sent Dee upstairs after a few hours, put her into the regular bed, and proceeded to do the necessary things for treating patients. There were several different doctors involved. One doctor told me they wanted me to stay there with Dee all the time, and for me to get some fluid into her, as much as I could. Coffee, water, fruit drinks, tea, anything, to get fluids in her. There is a type of bench built in along the wall in the rooms in the new hospital. You can pull it out, and make it into a small bed. I was able to lie down, and sleep there for a while each night. I did go home shortly after Dee arrived in the room, to feed the kitties, and get my toothbrush, razor, and clean clothes. This took me about an hour. While Dee was in the hospital, about every 2 hours, someone would come in to check her, and do the usual blood pressure, temperature, etc. They worked on the left foot heel while she was in the ER room. From then on they then changed the bandages on her foot twice daily.

I proceeded to give Dee coffee, juices, water, tea, anything I could get her to drink. And I stayed with her all the time. I only went home once a day to care for the kitties, check the mail and get fresh clothes, then I would go back to the hospital to be with Dee. I would go to the hospital cafeteria to get sandwiches, drinks, etc. for myself. I always brought different things for Dee to eat, from the cafeteria: yogurt, soda, whatever looked good that I thought Dee would eat. We were slowly getting life back into Dee. The hospital also furnished food for her too.

Dee recovered pretty quickly. I know Dee recognized me,

and she knew I was trying to help her. Dee was in the hospital, from Nov. 16 to Nov 21st. 2017. Kaiser took very good care of Dee, and was able to get her pretty much back to her old self, except for the blister on her left foot heel! We (the ambulance crew and I) took her to our home, and put her in a hospital bed, in our dining room. I had helpers come to help me care for Dee eight hours per day, until January 28, 2018. By then, we had her walking a little, and I was caring for the blister on her foot every day. I was able to take care of Dee's needs after the helpers left each day. Many people thought Dee would not make it back to walking. But I was determined Dee should regain some walking ability. Yes, she had limited walking, but up till now she has done pretty good. It took fifteen months of doctoring to finally get that heel healed up and it has given us many problems since the first incident. It had a problem again about six months later, but it recovered. It came back in November of 2019. I am working on it daily now, to try to get it healed again. It seems, heel wounds are the hardest part of the body to get healed, and take the longest time.

After a while, in 2018 we were able to take Dee outside for fresh air, and to take walks around the block. At first we used a wheelchair, but then after a while she was able to use a regular four wheeled walker. She could walk around the block, always with someone walking with her as she was not very stable. Because our house is small, I also purchased a three wheeled walker for Dee to use here in the house. It folds a little to get through the small doorways. Things were going along pretty good, but Dee did fall down a couple times. She did not get hurt from those falls and I was always able to get Dee up on her feet again. One time an Oakland police officer helped me get Dee back on her feet. After Dee seemed to be doing so well, and after more than a year at home, I purchased a stand up walker. The concept seemed to me to be just what Dee needed. Dee used it daily for about a week, but then on June 4th, 2019, she had a fall.

We had gone out for a walk with it two times but this time, out on our driveway, Dee somehow got her foot under the walker wheel, or stepped on the wheel, I am not sure which, even though I was beside her. When Dee fell, I was on the opposite side of her. I saw her start to fall, but I could not reach her while she was falling. Dee fell on her right side and banged her head on the cement pavement. Right away, I could see a knot protruding about a quarter inch, on the right side of her skull. I had already called 911. I was holding Dee's head, and Dee was holding on to my hand and the fence when the Fire Department people arrived. The thing that really had me scared was that Dee had had a little piece of her skull removed when she had an aneurysm in 1996. This bump was very close to the area of the missing skull. The EMT people came, and took Dee to Kaiser, where they looked her over, and found a little bleeding on the brain from the bump. They kept her there overnight in the Emergency Room, to make sure there was no further bleeding. Luckily, everything was OK. I brought her home in our car the next morning. Then I called the stand up walker people and returned the walker. It was still under warranty. I never wanted to try that walker again, it was not a good fit for Dee, even though I had thought it could have been. Since then I have always been afraid of Dee's falling!! Over the years, Dee has stumbled many times. I am sure the drop foot is the main cause for all her falls.

I treated Dee's feet wounds every day with the required treatments the doctors had assigned and we went to see the doctor regularly. We treated the feet, and the blister all through 2018, and it finally seemed to be healed by March of 2019. That was good, except a small blister came on in the same location in June of 2019. This blister was minimal, and was gone after about two weeks. I never knew for sure how Dee could develop blisters like this until, one night in November of 2019, her feet went crazy in bed while she was sleeping. Dee always had active feet while she was sleeping in bed. I have experienced many kicks over the years.. But this night, Dee had no socks on, and her feet just kept going from side to side. I was asleep most of the night. But I awoke a couple times that night, and her feet were just going back and forth, Dee was still sound asleep. Everything seemed OK the next morning, and Dee walked about the same as she had been walking before. Well, a day or two after that, the blister came back again, and it was pretty big, not small at all. This must be how Dee acquired these blisters, by sliding her feet back and forth on the sheets during the night, with no socks on. This is probably the same thing that happened, while she was staying at the assisted living facility. I called Dee's doctor, and explained exactly what happened. We had to restart the treatment on the foot blister again.

Somehow, along about this time, Dee developed a sore spot on her right foot, where a bone sort of protrudes a little. This is how Dee's feet have grown over time, with just her unusual bone structure. Since then I have been treating both of these wounds and sending pictures to her doctor about every two weeks. Foot wounds take such a long time to heal for everyone, as I mentioned before. We see the doctor whenever they ask us to come in. As of this day, I am still treating these wounds. The blister is improving, but the sore on the right foot is giving me problems. The blister must be sore, and cause Dee pain when she walks. Dee's walking is failing, but I try to keep her doing some. One day at a time. But Dee is the Love of my Life, and I want to take as good of care of her as I can. We have an appointment to check on Dee's feet again. It's hard for the doctor and for me, but we have managed to help the foot heal.. Kaiser is extremely helpful.

Dee's Doing

These are some of the things Dee does, things she has always done. They mean so very much more to me at this stage in her life. They always make me happy and melt my heart. Dee tries to snuggle, sort of rolls over, while we are in bed. Sometimes she tries to talk to me, as I am getting her out of bed. I know she is trying hard to tell me something, but I cannot understand her language. Dee has not been able to talk understandably for a few years. I feel so sad, because she is trying to tell me something, as hard as she can. Dee squeezes my hand, and I know she is sending her love to me. I try to listen as best I can. I usually say OK, OK. That seems to make her happy. She tries to pick up her feet when I am trying to put her clothes on, or her shoes, or her special socks. Sometimes Dee looks at me, and starts laughing, because she sees me laughing. I try to talk to Dee, and she usually listens, unless there is food in front of her. Dee will eat almost any kind of food I put in front of her. But I have to watch her closely, she will try to eat napkins, paper towels, etc.. I always have to make sure there is nothing within her reach on the table. Otherwise she may pull things over to her, and try to eat them. Why couldn't it be me with Alzheimer's disease and then be allowed to die in my sleep?

The Dee that I met, and fell in love with 54 years ago, she is still in there! That Dee is still in there for sure, only covered with this Alzheimer's Disease. My love for Dee is stronger now than it has ever been. I know Dee cannot do anything for herself, she is completely dependent on me or one of my helpers to care for all her needs. It breaks my heart to see her struggle so much with this disease. I want to help Dee. I only wish I could help her recover her thinking, talking, and some of her other physical abilities.

Dee's Decisions

These are some decisions Dee has made that have changed our lives. Of course we both agree, after talking things over, but the original idea was all Dee's. In 1969, Dee said she wanted to move back to California from Indiana. I agreed. In May 1969, we made the move, and found an apartment in Alameda, Ca.. In July of 1970, she wanted us to move from Alameda, Ca., to Oakland, Ca..We moved. In August 1971, Dee saw our truck, and wanted me to buy it, which we did. In August 1971, we looked at this house, and she wanted us to buy it. We did. Dee wanted me to buy the Nova in November, 1978. We did. In late 1993, I explained the mileage on our old Nova, and felt it was getting tired. The old Nova had 165,000 miles on it. We did not want to get stranded somewhere with a car breakdown. Dee and I purchased a new Buick automobile in January 1994. Then Dee wanted a new refrigerator. We purchased a new one. At about that same time, we replaced the plumbing in our house, (2002), and I also replaced the kitchen sink and cabinets. Dee picked out the sink, counter top and colors. Dee has the ability of color matching. I wanted all this to make it easier for Dee and it improved the appearance and the ease of working in the kitchen, preparing our food. We installed new vinyl windows in 2003. It made the house much warmer. We put in a central heating system in 2012. As we are both getting older, heat in the winter is more enjoyable. As Dee's disease was taking a greater toll on her, I decided we needed to upgrade our bathroom. This was 2018. We had a bathtub, and we took that out and installed a shower and new bathroom sink. This change made it so much easier and safer for Dee's bathing. One of our helpers suggested we do this; I had never thought of doing this. I have also, over time, purchased additional handicapped equipment to help with Dee. Walkers, a bigger transport chair, a ramp, a shower seat, a shower chair, etc. Another helper told me about the shower chair. I have been able to find different supplies for Dee's care. Dee has never complained about anything we purchased. One other thing I just thought of, it was probably 45 years ago when Dee saw a carpet with flower designs on it. Dee wanted it, and it has been on our living room floor for all these years. Many people have commented about it. Yes, we have made many, many purchases of many things over the 53 years we have been married. Dee is the Love of My Life, and there is nothing I would not try to get, or do for her. Dee is my Love!!

Health Care Coverage

Dee worked at Kaiser Oakland for 26 years. One of her benefits was health coverage. Excellent health coverage for sure. Not many companies offer this type of coverage to their employees now. But the Kaiser doctors have always taken excellent care of Dee. Dee had that aneurysm, a broken ankle, a broken hip, a broken back, and now another broken ankle, the right leg this time. They are doing surgery to help it heal and allow Dee to walk again. Her walking was limited, and probably will remain limited, but if Dee can walk some and be able to stand, that is about all I can hope for. While Dee is in the hospital, I worry about her and her care, but most of all, I just miss her. I often think of what my life would be like if Dee were to pass from this world. It certainly is not a subject I want to think about. Dee is always in my prayers, and has been every day that I have known her.

We will never know, but I have always felt Dee's health problems came about when she lived with her stepmother. Dee had to live with the step mother for about 4 to 5 years, when she had severe malnutrition, along with very poor hygiene practices. Dee had to wear tattered clothing and shoes that were always too small. I believe that eating lima beans three times a day, for months and years, when she was a child, had taken its toll on Dee's future health. Living in a condemned building with no running water or heat, would make survival difficult too. My knowledge about Dee's childhood has really made me appreciate my childhood. I had to work hard but I always had nutritious food to eat, plenty of food, clean clothes and a clean and warm bed. I was not spoiled, but after learning about Dee's upbringing, I know I was very lucky. I know nothing can ever be done to correct this situation, but I Love my Dee!! I will always take care of my Love!

Early in July of 2020 Dee broke her right ankle. On the 1st of July at 10 pm EMS took her to Kaiser ER. Because of the Corona virus, I could not go with her. But then I was called several times that night by the Kaiser doctors. The surgery to repair the ankle was supposed to be done on July 3rd but the doctor called me and said they could not do the surgery because of Dee's sodium level. Because Dee's sodium was low, they put off the surgery until the next day. They did the surgery the next morning, Saturday, July 4th, 2020, on Dee's foot. Then the doctor called me and said that Dee had had some heart complications at some point while on the operating table. I did not know what her condition was at this point, but they asked me to come and visit her that day, after she had been moved back to her room. They wanted me to come to visit, even though we were restricted from visiting because of the Corona virus. The doctor cleared it with the Security team. After the call, around noon I went to see Dee. She was in the bed, hooked up to a monitor, IV, catheter, etc.. The nurses were checking on Dee every few minutes. I am sorry to say that Dee looked so absolutely terrible, I was afraid she was going to die. However, knowing the toughness of Dee, she has always kept on going! After the visit I went home and wondered and worried about Dee and whether I would be able to visit her again in the hospital,

    While I was visiting the hospital, a Kaiser doctor talked to me about what to do with Dee. I said maybe I should put her in a home. The doctor explained to me, they (Kaiser Doctors) really wanted me to take her home, for me to care for her here at our house. The doctor was very clear, they (Kaiser) wanted Dee to come back to her own home. I agreed, as I know she would not make it very well in a strange place. Kaiser ordered a hospital bed for our house, a hydraulic lift, home health nurse, physical therapy, and speech therapist. They said I would need to hire extra help, to help me care for Dee at home. The rest of the supplies I have, and can replenish. Dee came back to our house. The wonderful thing is, Dee is responding positively to her care here although I am not sure about Dee's mental capacity at this point.

    It has been about two months now. I am doing my best to take good care of Dee. It appears to me that Dee must have had a stroke at some point. Probably on the operating table, as that is where the doctor said they had the most trouble. But they were able to bring her back, without needing to do CPR. Dee is more alert and I think she knows me. But Dee cannot talk or even make sounds from her mouth. I can get her to stick out her tongue some, but no sounds. Dee's right leg has no strength at all, but her left leg has a little resistance when I try to exercise it. Dee's right hand has a little strength, but her left hand is still very strong, it is hard to break her grip, it is so very strong. The left hand wants to grip on to anything and everything. As time is moving along, I have learned things to do to block the grip. For one, I roll up a washcloth, tape it together, and put those in her hands to hold on to. Without that, she will make it difficult to move, or to do things with her. The physical therapists suggested this. Dee has to wear diapers all the time. And I try to keep her on a schedule of changing the diaper every 3 or 4 hours. I do not know if Dee can hear anything. I have rung a bell beside her ears, and there seems to be no response. We (my helpers and I), are able to give Dee a shower/bath each Wednesday of the week. But we wash her up well every morning, while she is lying in bed. We put towels under her and move her from side to side to make sure she is always clean. I always want to make sure that Dee does not get any sores or rashes. Cleanliness is extremely important.

When Dee first came home from the hospital on July 6th, 2020, we were having trouble with her blood pressure. It was running very high. I have been monitoring it every day, and I send the results to her doctor about every two weeks. It was very high at first, and a little unstable for a while, but her pressure is pretty regular now. I discovered part of the reason for her pressure being very high. Dee used to hold the grip in her left hand very tightly and that is the arm we use for the blood pressure testing. Now, after we have Dee washed for the day, we put the blood pressure cup on her left arm, put a pillow under her arm, and then remove whatever she is holding in her hand. Dee usually sleeps for a while after washing. It is stressful for her to take her blood pressure, I am sure. After she sleeps a little, I press the button, and the machine does the measuring. I record the measurements on a sheet of paper in the kitchen, to be able to send that information to her doctor, as he requested. Then I e-mail them to her doctor. The electronic medical charts are more efficient than needing to write everything down, like we had to do years ago.

The rest of the day for Dee is spent watching cartoons, westerns, and other shows on her TV. Some days Dee is very consumed by the cartoons, and some days not. It seems to me, she likes to watch the movements. I am not sure if part of her hearing has come back. It does not appear that it has. But Dee's movement of her head from left to right, and somewhat up and down, and the tapping of her left foot on the floor while she is sitting in her chair, all that has improved. Dee is trying to make sounds from her mouth, but cannot manage much more than a sigh and or moan. Dee's eyes seem to be very alert, they follow me and our helpers around, as we move around the bed, attending to her needs. Dee overall has improved tremendously since coming home from the hospital this last time, on July 6th. I only hope she will continue improving. Dee seems to be making a minute amount of change each day.

More on Dee's Past

My Dee worked as a waitress for 18 years, during the first part of her working career. Then she worked as a receptionist for 26 years. From what Dee has told me about her past life, she graduated from high school at age 18, out of a class of 350 students. Her aunt required her to be on the honor roll, as much as Dee was able. Dee told me she was on the honor roll at Irvington High School several times. And before high school, the Nuns in her younger school years said Dee was a good student. I wonder if all this may have put a lot of stress on her mind and her memory. My reason for thinking this is that after we were married, and she worked as a waitress, Dee could remember exactly what items of food the customer ordered And of course, she learned many of the customers names and probably more, such as where they worked, their families, what city they may have lived in, etc.. Dee had a terrific memory. Waitresses seem to have that in common. And they take an interest in their returning customers. Remembering and recalling all this exact information seems to me would create a lot of stress on a person's brain. Yes, we all remember things, but Dee always seemed a little excessive in remembering things. And when she was working as a receptionist, it was almost the same as waitress work. She always worked with people, talking with them, watching how they paid, how much they paid, and gathering a lot more information about why they were in the medical facility and for what kind of help. Dee was always so precise, and efficient, although many times I recall that her cash did not come out correctly. Dee would have to find out where she might have made a mistake. This could happen while she was working as a waitress, or while working as a receptionist. If there was a monetary problem, she would go back and recall every transaction from that day. It was stressful I am sure, as some days, she might have handled over 100 people. That is a lot to remember. I would try to help her, but she would not let me deal with money that was not mine. This was her responsibility, she said. Kaiser had rules concerning handling their money. For all of Dee's working career, she needed to stress her mind every single day. From what Dee has told me over time, she started working as a waitress right after graduation. And I know she worked as a waitress in Newark, New Jersey, and in New York City. Then she moved to the west coast, and started working as a waitress in Hollywood. California. And of course I know what her career was like after we married. At first, I did not want Dee to work, but she just was adamant, she wanted to work for us, to bring in extra money. And she did not want to sit around the house, or apartment all the time. Dee wanted to be active. Dee has always been a very strong worker, confident, efficient, just a great worker. And Dee could fit in anywhere.

During her high school years in New Jersey, Dee was required to work for Prudential Insurance to pay for her upkeep, and supply her own clothing. Dee had to give half of her paycheck to her aunt for room and board, and she could keep the other half for supplying her own clothing, and her daily needs. But from what Dee has told me, Dee did not have much to spend on herself.

When she lived with the step mother, Dee suffered from malnutrition: no milk or calcium to help the body make strong teeth and strong bones. Then while living in New Jersey, working at Prudential Insurance, Dee had to go to the dentist every week.

Dee's teeth were so soft they would get cavities very easily. The dentist told Dee she needed to have all her teeth pulled, but he (male) would not do that, because of Dee being so young. Instead, he just kept filling them. Some teeth had fillings in fillings, Dee told me. Dee was on a sort of installment payment plan with the dentists. She just paid a certain amount each week, as she had to go to the dentist every week. I know Dee paid the dentist all she owed. I do not know much more about Dee's early problems with her teeth. This is only what she has told me. But I do know, when we were married, Dee was 29 years old, she had had her upper teeth pulled, and had a denture plate. She never told me what her age was or where she had her upper teeth pulled. But after we had been married for about three years and we were living in Alameda, California, we found a dentist to pull the remaining bottom teeth and immediately a lower denture plate was put in her mouth to replace her teeth. She has worn those same denture plates for all these years now. We did have to get the upper plate repaired several years ago, but that repair was done in one day. These dentures do not match, and never have. The top teeth do not align, not close to align with the bottom teeth to make a match. I wanted Dee to get a new set of dentures made many years ago, but Dee did not want any new plates. I think her reason was that new dentures cause sore spots on the patient's gums. I am aware of how much pain Dee suffered with the bottom plate when she had the lower teeth pulled. And if you ask denture wearers, food particles get under the dentures, and the gums grow and change over time and that can also cause sore gums. I wish Dee had gotten correct fitting dentures years and years ago. Now , because she uses dentures to eat, I have to clean them each morning and night. I put them in her mouth each morning, and take them out each night. Sometimes I need to clean them during the day, as food collects under, and behind them. I always have to watch her swallowing, to make sure she swallows and does not choke. Frequently, she coughs, after drinking fluids, probably because the fluid goes down the wrong place in her throat. But Dee has a tendency to hold water in her mouth, and sometimes slosh it around before swallowing. I have to always be on the lookout for choking. Sometimes she holds food in her mouth, so I always try to cut her food into small pieces, especially meat, to prevent swallowing difficulties. When I make food ahead, I try to prepare things that are healthy, with low fat and easy to make in portions, any size I want, for feeding to Dee. I usually have a main dish and a salad or vegetable to go along with the meal, always with something good to drink. We do not go hungry. I do not make much as far as desserts, as we do not want the extra calories.

Alzheimer's Disease.

Dee was diagnosed with Alzheimer's disease in September 2006. Since that time I have read, and learned a tremendous amount about the disease, and its effects. It sneaks up on people, and they do not realize it until it's probably too late to properly prepare, although I do not know if anyone can prepare for Alzheimer's disease. It is the biggest thief, nothing can rob a person of anything and everything more than this disease does. I cannot imagine how it must feel to the person who has it. I only know what it does after someone is diagnosed with it. It is amazing how many people have it today. Maybe it was just called Senility in past years. I am not sure how much age has to do with it. Young and old seem to suffer from it. I think a lot of us older people get it, but usually pretty late in our lives. There is some help available for affected people, but no one seems to know how to cure it. Yes, research is working on it heartily, but it is a tough one to figure out. Research on this disease must be a nightmare! I donate to Alzheimer's Research.

Scientists have learned much from people's brains, the brains of people who have died with this disease. This disease causes Dee to have seizures sometimes. I give her medication every night to keep the seizures away. Hopefully, someone someday will find a cure for this terrible disease.

Some facilities will take care of patients with this disease, but all they can do is help these individuals make it through the day. They can feed them, get them to the bathroom, help them dress, wash them, etc. A few organizations offer help, but from all I have learned about them, they will take the patient and babysit them day after day and watch their behavior, but none have explained to me any direction anyone can go, which could offer some understanding and a way to offer memory development. I realize the disease affects the brain, but I have always hoped someone could help me teach my spouse some way to show her, for example the A's, B's, and C's. Repetition is what I have been told, which I try to do, but I am hoping to find other ways to help my wife communicate. No one that I know of, has a magic pill that will reverse or cure this disease. If you go to your doctor with a broken finger, usually they can fix it somehow, and the person can go on with their usual routine after it heals. Alzheimer's is not that kind of problem/disease. It just never heals. I commend the caretakers who work with patients who have this disease. It requires a tremendous amount of patience. I speak from my own experience! If the patient does something that seems wrong, or causes messes and cannot follow directions, you cannot get angry with them. They are innocent. The brain waves are not making contact. They do not get angry at you. I wonder if they somehow think we care givers, could be the crazy ones. I will always be patient with my Dee.

My lovely wife Dee has had a diagnosis of Alzheimer's for 14 years now. And as I stop and think hard about different things, things that happened years and years ago, I wonder where it started. Some researchers think bad teeth may have caused it's onset at some point in a person's life. And I wonder how much diet plays a part in this disease process. And I wonder, exactly when the disease actually begins in a person. I know from what Dee has told me, after she left her grandmother's care, and moved in with the step mother, Dee's nutrition changed drastically. Dee said the step mother had very little money. I do not know why Dee's father was not supplying the family with food, and money to buy food to keep going. I think the step mother was not willing to get a job, or do anything to earn money for food. Dee did tell me the step mother spent money on makeup supplies. And for sure, there was a great shortage of love, after Dee was taken away from the Palaskas grandmother. I do not think there was much love for Dee, at the Aunt's house in New Jersey, either. Dee must have been an unwanted burden for the Aunt. I imagine Dee was strong minded at times, but with all the abuse Dee suffered, I may have felt the same way too. But Dee did strive to pay her own way, while living with the Aunt, and her family. I never knew the ages of the Aunt's children, whether Dee was older, or about the same age. Dee's Aunt Pat, was the oldest of the female Palaskas children. Dee's father John, was the oldest of the six children.

 I really began to worry about Dee for a year or two before she was diagnosed with Alzheimer's. Dee used to ask me for a lot of information, information which she used to be able to remember. I wondered just exactly what was happening. I know myself, I forget names, and dates, and different things that were important to me at one time. But I think that is somewhat normal, we all forget things at one time or another. Now, I write everything of importance on the calendar, in our kitchen. Each morning, I glance at it to see what importance may be happening that specific day. I know I may not remember, so I just write things down. I also keep a close account of our checkbooks, savings accounts and our charge accounts too. Because I have forgotten in the past to write down deposits, withdrawals, and once in a while, checks. We have had a couple purchases, where the company withdrew the charged amount, and it was directly withdrawn from our accounts. This was so hard! That day of the month would come, and I would forget to write it in the register. Then the balance would be off. Each time I do any transaction at the bank now, I ask for a balance. I do remember that from the first year of our marriage, 50 some years ago, Dee could not be responsible for taking care of any of our banking accounts.

The first few years after Dee was diagnosed, we went to many places ,and I even had some golf outings when Dee would go with me. But as time moved along, I got to the place where I felt I could not trust her. She never did wander away, but too many of the things she would do just made me feel uncomfortable. If we were going somewhere and I needed to leave Dee for a while, I would ask someone there to keep an eye on her and not let her wander off. Dee did wander around some, but someone would catch her, bring her back, and watch her until I returned. If there were a bunch of people around, they sort of kept an eye out, especially after they knew of her illness. I never did lose her. One time here at home, I do not know where I was, but I know I was home, out in the garage I think. Dee went out of the house and wandered up the street to Herman's house. Herman knows about Dee's illness. and so he called me. Luckily, all our neighbors now know of Dee's illness. For a few years I would go out golfing with a group of guys, on Monday mornings. For quite some time, I would leave Dee here by herself, this was before her memory was getting too bad. Each time I came home, she seemed to have been ok. I was concerned about her turning on the kitchen stove, or leaving the house, etc., but she never did, except for the one time she went to Herman's house, but I had not been golfing that day. Then after some time, I would ask Carol to come and watch Dee while I went out golfing. After some time, I had to stop the Monday morning group.

I would meet up with a couple people on Friday mornings and Carol would stay with Dee. I always played the short courses, which would allow me to be back home after about 3 hours. As time changed and the amount of time I wanted to spend golfing, it just became too risky. And it was not relaxing at all. Besides, I have always worried about Dee, even though I knew someone was with her. After a little more time went by, I stopped golfing, I decided to give it up completely. Dee was so much more important to me than golf. But I really miss playing golf.

I believe it was sometime early in 2016 when I started looking for help, for my caring for Dee and her illness. I followed up a few suggestions I had been given by Kaiser. Alameda County Health Services, and others, whose names and titles I had picked up. There were some organizations who came to our house, and sort of looked at the severity of Dee's condition. They came to let me know when, and where I could find companies, or organizations who care for Alzheimer's patients. One of the first questions asked of me was about our eligibility for Medicare or Medicaid. We do have medical coverage through Kaiser Medical Facility and Medicare, but that is all. We cannot get any other coverage or help from any government organization because a household with assets worth more than $50,000, net worth, are not eligible. The value of a person's home, or real estate is not counted in that sum. It is just the amount you have in the bank or something that can be turned into cash quickly, or things like bonds. Dee and I have saved all our lives, and we now have more than that amount accumulated in our bank. When I told these organizations this, they told me we did not qualify. And that seemed to limit who could help, and who could offer help. No one offered help, but they suggested organizations I could contact who might help me care for Dee, with her condition. That would have meant I would have had to move Dee from our home, into a different home for her and I would have had to pay for their services. I do not object to paying, but there was only one option that seemed to fit what I was looking for. Moving Dee out of her home here did not appeal to me at all. I decided I was always going to keep Dee here in this house with me.

To get some relief, just for a few hours at a time, I was taking Dee to a place, which cared for Alzheimer's patients, in Berkeley, California. I believe this was in 2015. This organization has a few different locations, but I chose the Berkeley location, mostly because it is probably the closest to our home. It was not that I wanted someone to try to help Dee, I only wanted someone to watch her, someone who was different from me, in the hope of getting some of Dee's memory to return and also just to help her. They have different classes all during the day to help patients make crafts, do some singing, and they have different ideas to try to help people with their memory. This is a really super great place, and they do take very good care of the people they care for. They have a remarkable staff. It is not an overnight facility. I would take Dee there about 9am, and come back to pick her up around 3pm. This facility has a schedule of classes they teach each day, plus they feed the patients and make sure they are escorted to the bathroom and each person's movements are recorded. Some of the staff sing, play music and play games. Trivia was big, but many people were unable to respond to the subject. I could take Dee there 5 days a week if I wanted, but I did not want to do that. I chose to take Dee there on Mondays, Thursdays and some Saturdays. I am not sure if Dee enjoyed being there or not. She always seemed to be happy to see me when I came to pick her up. The staff helped the residents make crafts and had wonderful ideas.. They made simple little items for Halloween, Thanksgiving and Christmas, plus weekly ideas. The staff usually sent these items, which the residents made, home with them. We have a few here in our house. All items have a purpose. I love them!

    I had Dee on this schedule for about three years. But then I needed to go back east to check on our property. I had Dee take a break in November 2016, and then Dee was back attending afterwards. In October of 2017, I notified the people there, at this daily day care center, that Dee would be taking another break, as I was going to put her in the same assisted living facility for about 4 weeks. I had plans to travel back east to visit family, work on the properties, and travel to Dee's home, where she was born and where she lived the early years of her life. My plans for Dee, was to leave her in the assisted living facility from October 23rd, to November 16th, 2017. Because of the many complications from that stay, Dee has never been able to get back to the Berkeley organization. It is so sad because Dee's health and mobility will not allow for this now. Things have just happened that way, but I still have my Dee, the Love of my life. I truly wish Dee was healthy enough to go back, because the staff there are so caring! I hope they are all doing well, and safe.

There was a period, a few years ago, where Dee would start yelling. For no reason at all. It was the Alzheimer's disease. We could be sitting watching a television program, and she would yell at the top of her lungs. I do not know how she could get her voice to be that loud. I hoped she would not hurt herself, I mean her throat, but there was nothing I could do to stop her yelling. I had purchased a pair of the ear protectors, like headphones, for myself, but that did not help too much. It did help some when I tried sitting in a different chair, although her voice still sounded like she was sitting next to me. It really made it hard to watch any programs on the television. I have no idea where her yelling came from, nor what may have caused it. Yes, I did my best to try to ignore her and the yelling, but I was afraid the neighbors would think I was hurting her. But sometimes the neighbors would come for a visit, and she would start yelling while they were here. After a while, people knew what was happening. If the phone rang, I would have to take the call to the back room, or outside. And the yelling would come and go, but

I never knew when it would happen. I really had to watch Dee, while we were in church. Many times, I felt it was coming on, so I would put my mouth very close to Dee's ear, talk to her for a few seconds, and she seemed to calm down. But the last time, when we had gone to the 8am service, I felt we had to get up and leave the church, as she would have disturbed everything. When we attended this other church, which is close to our home, the service was for all the sick people. The people there knew that most of the congregation was sick with all kinds of ailments, and they paid very little notice to Dee. After we had been attending several services, some ladies tried to offer Dee help. This was so kind of them. They offered Dee water, cake, cookies, orange juice, etc.. But Dee could not be trusted, as she would reach into the container, and would take a handful of cookies, or cake. I would stop her, then I would take something for Dee, and hand it to her. I really like this specific church, and I hope someday, we will be able to attend some services there again. We had attended a lot of activities there, long before Dee became ill. Dee and I always liked this church. I wish Dee and I could have steadily attended this church, back in the late 90's. But it was much too far for the friends in Alameda to travel, that is why we stayed with the church in Alameda. Now all those friends are now deceased and so we have no reason to stay with that church in Alameda. But we will attend both churches whenever I can.

Driving the car with Dee in it and yelling was a terrible thing to experience. She would be so loud. Sometimes I would put the window down, because the sound was so loud and disturbing. It made it very difficult to concentrate on the things ordinary driving of a car involves. It really made me become a defensive driver, looking for any situations which might possibly occur because Dee's yelling was so very distracting. Luckily, we never had to drive by any police, as I think they may have stopped me, to find out what was happening.

We have always eaten out over our lifetime together, and it

got to the point, we could only patronize one restaurant, mainly because we could sit over to the side, away from most of the other customers. I always tried to keep Dee occupied with something. The waitress, Emily, had gotten to know us from the many times we had been there to eat over the years before Dee became ill. Emily would bring Dee a cup of some kind of soup as soon as we could get seated. That would occupy Dee for a few minutes. We always used to drink coffee, but after a while, I ordered ice tea for Dee. Dee could spill most any kind of drink. I kept the tea close to me so I could take it and reach over the table, then put the straw next to Dee's lips, so she could take a sip and drink. Another thing Dee was doing is she would feed herself with her fingers. That was kind of tough. I decided to sit across the table, or as close to her as I could get, and feed her. That is the main reason why we patronized only this one restaurant. I did not want to embarrass Dee or others while we were eating there. At first, we used napkins for bibs, but Carol brought a couple bibs for Dee's use, and I started using them. Now we have to use the bibs all the time. Now, Dee cannot feed herself, nor do anything to help with any of her daily needs. As I mentioned before, over the years, Dee and I ate at so many wonderful restaurants. Emily treated us like royalty.

2020

This year, 2020, we have had this terrible Corona Virus and because of it, we cannot eat out anymore. However I am able to prepare some meals, which I try to make nutritious, relatively low calorie entries. I am not good at cooking, but making different things does have its rewards. I experiment a lot. I look at whatever I think I like, and try to make something interesting, tasty, and satisfying from that. As I have watched some of the cooking shows on television, I can see some of these chefs experimenting with different spices, ingredients, etc. Whatever they make looks good and appetizing to me. I used to bake a lot, but not any more, as Dee needs to lose some weight. I could lose a few pounds too. We are lucky enough to have neighbors and friends who bring in some food for us on occasions. I know Dee's illness would make it extremely difficult to get out now so I appreciate any help offered, no matter what kind of help that may be. I have helpers to help me each day, for which I pay. But if a neighbor offers to watch Dee for a few minutes, I appreciate them, and their offer but I do not want to take advantage of anyone. No, I do not go out to eat myself, but many times I will bring food home for Dee and myself and for anyone else who may be watching Dee for me. There are so many really good restaurants around that prepare food to go. That makes it convenient. But I do not like to eat restaurant food too often, it has salt, which can cause blood pressure to rise. Dee and I are healthy, and I want to keep it that way.

Dee's Feet

Some of these things about Dee's feet I have mentioned before. But again, Dee's feet have always been happy feet, this is how I describe them. From the beginning of our marriage, while Dee is sleeping in bed, her feet have moved, kicking around about all the time, but only when she is sound asleep. Yes, I have gotten used to it. But if her toenails are long, or sharp, it can wake me quickly! I am sure that is how the recent blisters have occurred. I believe Dee kept sliding her feet back and forth over the bed sheets, on the bed mattress, with no socks on or protection on her feet. The skin on Dee's feet seems pretty thin to me. It was never a problem until recently. I do not know why Dee's feet did not develop sores years ago. Maybe this was because before Dee would move more around the bed, roll over and sometimes put her feet on top of my legs, so she did not acquire any blister problems. But Dee has always had foot problems. Years ago, she was always buying shoes that were too small, but I did not know it. I wondered why Dee was always complaining about her shoes. Waitresses do a lot of walking. When Dee was working at waitress work, we used to have a neighbor who worked at a shoe store in downtown Oakland. One day we went to the store where he worked, and I asked him to measure Dee's feet to find out why Dee always seemed to have the same problems with her feet. We found out Dee's feet are a size 11 1/2, and narrow. So you can see, a size 10 shoe will not fit well. Dee was always buying size 9's and 10's. A size 10 men's shoe is close to what she needed, but of course she wore ladies shoes. From that time until now, we have ordered her shoes, ladies shoes, because stores usually do not carry those large sizes for women. For many years now, Dee has had no problems with her feet. But as time has moved along, she has developed callouses, especially after she acquired the drop foot. We are constantly fighting the callouses. Dee's feet are basically two sizes, the left foot is very narrow, but the right foot is closer to medium. To make a single pair of shoes work, we would buy the 11 1/2 medium, and put extra heel padding in the left shoe. That worked for years. However, when Dee acquired the drop foot, she had to start wearing a brace on her left foot, to raise the toe up, because the nerves and muscles could not operate the foot correctly. This required her to wear a larger shoe. The brace has to fit inside the shoe, to do what is necessary to raise the toe and to keep Dee from tripping. Dee has tripped so many times over the years. This is why, when we would be walking, I would always lock our arms together. Many times, the shoe would catch on something and she would start to fall, but I could catch her. Sometimes she would fall, but she did not go down hard. It usually only happened if the pavement surface was a little uneven. But then in June of 1998, Dee started to chase our kitty, slipped on the rug, and her left foot hit the table, breaking her ankle. Dee showed no sign of pain, because of the severed nerve in her back, from the epidural. I called 911. The EMT's could not understand how Dee could have such a broken, crooked foot, and not be in severe pain. Then they took Dee to Kaiser, and the doctor did surgery, and put a plate and pins in her ankle to stabilize it. Dee had to walk on crutches for a while, and she had a terrible time. Dee is not very well coordinated. We managed, as the doctor had put a medical boot on that foot until it healed. Then it was back to wearing the shoe with the brace. Luckily, Dee was not working as a waitress then. I do not know how she could have handled that. She recovered pretty well, but two years later, she stepped on her shoe lace, lost her balance, fell, and broke her left hip. Kaiser did surgery again, put a pin in her hip bone, along with screws to hold it in place. Then Kaiser said Dee suffers from Osteoporosis. This can be a problem for some women, but in Dee's case, I am sure her malnutrition as a child caused it mostly, or at least added to this problem. Now you can see why Dee's walking has always been something of a concern.

Along with the feet problem, just a couple other notes: Dee fainted in church in 2012. As she fell, her buttocks hit the pew as she was falling, and broke at least three vertebrae in her back. She had no surgery, and has not had any problems since it has healed. And now, believe me, I feel so sorry for Dee, and all the medical problems she has had to overcome. I only hope I have not been responsible for causing her any harm. I always, as I do now, tried to look for all dangers which could jump up and cause any new problems. Our helper, just yesterday, spotted a possible twist of Dee's foot. I have now made changes to try to prevent any more damage to her poor body. Dee is a very special woman. I know I am lucky to know her and to be married to her!

Our years together

Dee and I have been married for 53 years now. And I think we have always had a sort of different relationship compared to other married people who I know. Dee has a personality that is a little different from most women. She said it was because of her father's influence when she was a young child. She says he treated her like a boy! He probably did, as she was the only baby in the Palaskas house at that time. I truly think John Pallard loved his daughter very much. Then Dee's mother died, and John remarried. It seems to me, the stepmother took over control of John's life, and he did not fight back. John probably put most of his efforts in his work, and his new children by the stepmother. Dee was called a dumb Pollock as a little girl, by the other kids at school. Dee would come home crying because the other kids called her this name. When she told her father, John stiffened Dee up; he told her to tell them, "I am not a dumb Pollock, I am a Lithwock". Meaning by this, Dee's ancestors were from Lithuania, and not Poland! Dee told the kids teasing her this, and Dee said this shut them up, and they did not call her this name anymore. All of this made Dee a very independent woman. Since Dee always had to make her own way independently, I feel this is why her personality was a little different. At the time I met her, I was searching for a woman who was a little different. And beautiful! A beautiful, beautiful woman was Dee! Dee passed all my requirements! There is not a single thing I would change about our relationship, as I think back on our lives together. I wish Dee's health could be better, but that is God's doing, and nothing anyone can do about that. So, different personality, yes, but we fit each other, and I am a happy man to have Dee as my spouse. I love her!

Dee's Driving

I was told by Dee many years ago about her experience driving an automobile. This is comical, but very serious to Dee. When Dee was in Irvington High School, she signed up for the driver's training class. Dee wanted to drive a vehicle because her father had the old WWII Jeep. Dee never told me how John acquired the Jeep. He and Dee rode around in it at times. I believe Dee said it was usually on Sundays. Dee said she had a blast riding in that Jeep, she and her father laughed all the time while they were in it. So Dee wanted to learn how to drive a car. Dee thought the driver's training class would be just the thing to teach her how to drive. Dee wanted to have fun driving around in a car of her own. Dee probably wanted to have a Jeep of her own. She said the car the school used for driver training was a 1955 Chevrolet. I think many schools used a '55 Chevrolet for these classes. One day, the instructor took Dee out, along with two boys. Dee said the boys did their turns driving, and then the instructor asked Dee to drive them back to the school. Dee was doing OK, until they came to the drive at the school. I never saw this, but I can only imagine the sight in my mind. Somehow the drive must have had some curves in it. As Dee was going forward, the instructor told Dee to drive straight ahead. Straight ahead was a pile of dirt, maybe gravel. But the instructor told Dee to go straight. Dee did as instructed. The car ran up on the pile of dirt, the instructor fell out of the car, and the car was severely damaged. The instructor was so angry, and asked Dee why did you do that? Dee told him,' "You said go straight ahead", and that is what I did.' Dee did not know! Dee was not allowed in the class again. And all the kids at school teased Dee, about wrecking the car. After that experience, Dee was terrified of driving a car. Dee was embarrassed, but it really was not her fault.

When we lived in Indiana for 14 months, we drove the '59 Chevrolet. I had put a trailer hitch on it to pull our trailer, the one I had made while in the Navy, in Alameda, in 1967. We towed that trailer to Indiana after I was discharged. While living in Indiana, we lived on a farm. We really needed a pickup truck, as I could not drive the car and trailer out in the fields. I purchased a 1949 Chevrolet pickup from a friend. It did not look like much, but it ran good. I drove it a lot. I wanted to teach Dee how to drive it. Dee had gotten her driver's permit. My mom and dad had a car with an automatic transmission, and Dee did pretty good driving it. But both our truck, and car were straight shifts, meaning you needed to use a clutch to change the gears, in order to move faster. I had taken Dee out in the field to learn how to drive the truck, and shift it too. Dee did pretty good. She became more acquainted with driving and shifting. I think Dee would have been a good driver. After a time she was able to drive the truck from our house to mom and dad's house, which was 1/2 mile away. Dee was getting more comfortable. All she had to do was watch out for other traffic. Country roads usually do not have much traffic, compared to city streets. We also had a wonderful dog. Dee would make the dog ride along with her. But Dee did not really want to drive, and I gave up on the idea of Dee's driving after we left Indiana. Over the years of our marriage, Dee asked me would I like for her to learn to drive, to help me when we were on long trips. No, I said, I could stop and rest if I needed to. Dee would never be able to relax when driving. I felt Dee never needed the extra stress!!

Dee's Walking

Of course Dee's walking now is very much compromised. But we do the best we can. Dee has fallen several times, and I do not want any more falls. We are currently treating a wound on her left hip, caused by a fall. We are treating a blister on her left heel, caused by rubbing her heel very hard on the bed sheets while she is asleep. We are treating a wound on her right foot, caused by a protruding bone. But we always walked a lot, it is good to walk and talk. Even today, we walk as much as we can. Dee and I loved to walk and talk with each other, even from day one of our marriage.

Walking for Dee has changed tremendously over her last 25 years. I mentioned before about Dee getting the epidural shot in 1995, which severely damaged the nerve in her back. That was the beginning of most of the walking problems. Prior to that time, we overcame the shoe problems by purchasing the correct kind, size, and type of shoes. The shoes at first looked more like men's shoes. But as time went along, we could see more and more women wearing the same kind of shoes that Dee was wearing. Dee thought they were old ladies shoes. But I kept telling her, it does not matter, if they fit, and are comfortable, it makes no difference what they look like. But this was in the 70's and 80's, when style mattered to Dee. Now, people wear almost anything. That is OK, if they like their shoes and they are comfortable. Most people wear sneakers nowadays. But Dee's size 12, and my size 10 are almost the same in overall size. I can wear Dee's shoes, but I could never fill them like Dee does. Dee's tripping had more to do with the drop foot than the shoes. I do not recall Dee tripping prior to the drop foot problem. But since that happened, I try my best to always hold her arm or hand, especially around steps, when walking and going up and down steps. When we would go grocery shopping, something I did not mind doing with Dee, I always made her push the cart, because she would then be holding the handle. That way she could catch her foot if it caught on a different surface. One time we were crossing the street, we were in the crosswalk, but I said let's start running. I was impatient. I had a hold of Dee's hand, and I started to go, but Dee said no, I cannot run. Before I could get stopped, Dee almost fell. I have always felt badly for Dee, and at myself for doing that! Dee could have injured herself, but she did not. I was thinking about something else at the time, and had forgotten about Dee not being able to run. I never, never tried anything like that again. This was a lesson well learned by me. Dee walked miles and miles while she was working as a waitress. We both have commented many times that it was a good thing she was not working as a waitress when she acquired the drop foot. Dee and I never directly blamed the doctor for causing Dee's drop foot, but it is such a shame that this happened to anyone, especially Dee.

Because of Dee's restricted walking capabilities, I decided to purchase a transport chair to help Dee get around more easily. For example, it took quite some time for Dee to cross the street. So many drivers are in such a hurry, and some almost ran us down! In order to make the situation easier for us, I purchased the transport chair. We now have three of them. This allows me to put Dee in the chair and push her wherever we need to go. If we have a doctor's appointment, we usually need to cross a wide and busy street. Luckily, I am able to walk pretty well, and I can go at a fairly good pace. And pushing Dee is no problem, except many people still do not respect handicapped people in wheelchairs. It seems it is the American way! A few years ago, Dee could walk around the block using her 4 wheeled walker. As her walking deteriorated, I used to push her in her transport chair, then she would stand and use the chair like a walker. But now all I can do is put her in the transport chair, and push her wherever we need to go. I realize that as people get older, sometimes our walking becomes more difficult. Dee's walking is now gone. I say this in respect, because after we both retired, we would walk up the street to the church services just about every day. The service was at 8am. And the walk is about one mile each way. It usually took us about 25 minutes to walk each way. And it was a good walk, mostly smooth sidewalks. We always crossed the street with the signal lights. The lights stop the automobile traffic. It was a really nice walk, and made us get out early in the mornings. I hope to make this trip this summer with Dee in her transport chair. I can push it that distance easily. Dee and I had a very good retirement planned. Sad, that we have not been able to enjoy it, the way we had planned, and hoped for.

The transport chairs have been a great help. When my mother passed away, we went back to Indiana to pay our respects. It was a sad time, but something we both wanted to do. To travel to Indiana from Oakland, California, it is necessary to fly if you need to get there quickly. The airports here are large and require lots of walking. And Indianapolis airport, the one we fly into, requires lots of walking too. We visited Indiana a few times, using this method. Our neighbor would take us to the BART railway system here, then I would put Dee in her chair, use the elevator to get to the trains and travel to and from the airports. All public travel around here is wheelchair accessible. We would board the train, I would lock the wheelchair's wheels, and we would go straight to the airport. After we used the airport elevators and checked in to get our tickets, we would go through the security system. Dee always stayed in her chair while the agents would run the wand across and around her. Then away we could go. Of course, I had to walk through the security monitor by myself. I could move Dee through the airports more quickly this way. We usually had to change planes half way through our trip. I would request the airlines to have a transport chair waiting for our flight, to move us to the next departing gate. This way I could still move Dee through the other airport quickly too. It was a little hard on boarding planes, but I always signed up to board first, ahead of most of the other passengers. I was able to get Dee out of the chair. Then I would walk backwards holding Dee's hands, and guide her to our seats. Using the bathroom on airplanes is something else. They are very small, but some have a curtain to pull around, which allows more space and privacy. We make it. We traveled to Indiana, via this method a few times. When we flew to the Indianapolis airport, the transport chair went with us on the plane, and the airline would bring it to the exit ramp when we arrived. I used it to get Dee through all airports. The one newer innovation at airports is the family bathrooms. They allow the whole family to use them together. Dee and I used them, they are very convenient. These are wonderful for handicapped travelers. There is plenty of space, and it's easy to use the toilet, and it's easy to wash our hands. Also it is pretty easy for me to change Dee's diapers. I can also brush my teeth.

Kitties

Dee always loved kitties. Maybe because, when she was a child in Scranton, there was an orange kitty which she loved to pet. She did not know who the kitty belonged to. But the kitty must have liked Dee, and Dee had found something that showed Dee unconditional love. I imagine that made a big impact on Dee at that time, when she probably was about 5 years old. Dee always described the kitty as a big orange kitty. It seems to me, Dee always remembered that feeling. And as I have said, the first kitty we had, came less than three months after we were married. Since that time, we have always had kitties. Usually more than one, and as many as nine. Today we have three. I have some pictures of our kitties, and some pictures with Dee holding and petting them. But words, and pictures cannot explain the feeling I get when I see Dee with these kitties. I can just see the adoration on Dee's face, it's like something comes over her at those moments. And the kitties always respond by purring loudly. I really think Dee must be remembering those moments in her early life with that orange kitty in Scranton. Maybe Dee was a kitty, in an earlier life? I used to have a bench beside our garage. When Dee would sit on it, it would not be but 30 seconds before a kitty would be perched on Dee's lap. Dee would sit and stroke that kitty for a long time, or until another one jumped on Dee's lap, and chased the first one off. We never had any fighting kitties. I would scold the aggressive one, and sometimes I would grab it and shake it, to be sure I had its attention, and then I would lecture it, saying, "You don't do that!". Then I would put it down, point at it, and say, "No fighting". Crazy enough, but that usually worked the first or second time, after I got their attention. Dee would look at me, and I would look at her, and I would say, "You want me to shake you too?" Then we both would laugh, and laugh at each other. Dee and I always had fun, at just about anything we did. Kids, and many other people started calling Dee "the cat lady". And Dee has been called that since the day after we moved to the rental house in Oakland, July 1970. Even the people Dee worked with, knew she loved kitties. Dee had a favorite at Kaiser that she called Oscar. The kitties we have had here at this house have all had their own names. We never had to go to the number system.

But I must confess, I had one which I had brought home from work. I was afraid he was going to be deaf, because of the circumstances when I found it. It was a small kitten, I thought it would be deaf, but I could not let it stay where it was. That kitty stayed here in our house for 18 years. Luckily he did not turn out to be deaf. He used to sleep with us every night, and he would curl up on my arm while I was sleeping. He liked Dee, but I think I was his favorite. I wish we could still have him, but he has been gone for 5 years now. It is crazy how we cannot forget animals, and the people we Love. We have had most of our deceased kitties cremated, and we have their little wooden boxes on a shelf in our closet. Dee and I have always said to each other, if we could win the lottery, we would buy land somewhere, and take in unwanted animals. Memories! We both love animals, and they offer so much friendliness, love, and affection, if we only let them. It is too bad many people will not have their animals spayed, or neutered. There are too many animals put to death each day in animal shelters. Too sad!

Yes, Dee loves her kitties. At one time we had 9 kitties living here. Most of them lived in the garage. Dee had toys for them to play with, blankets, and towels everywhere for them to sleep on, and plenty of food and water, fresh every morning and evening. We probably did not give them the best medical treatment, but we tried our best. I had made a cabinet for the back porch, with 2 tiers for sleeping, and partitioned areas too. We had kitties living on, and in this for years. We have an older cat living in one of the partitions now. I have remodeled it some, and it now has potted flower pots and other plants on top, but still room for kitties. I made this shelf out of scrap materials which I brought home when I worked at Del Monte. The plants on top at the moment are blooming orchids. Dee always loved flowers, especially blooming ones. And I have been pretty lucky at keeping them growing and blooming. We have a gardenia plant out front, and I bring in fresh blooms daily while it's blooming. We both love the aroma. Dee always made it easy for me to care for plants, flowers, and having a productive garden. Dee appreciated the aroma's from all the different kinds of plants. Dee makes life beautiful for me, and always has. Dee is my Love.

More About Dee's Alzheimer's

I had mentioned Alzheimer's disease before, but there are many many experiences I could tell you about Dee, and her disease. We are now starting her 15th year with the illness. It has gone through several stages. Yes, I was told these would come up, but it is hard to recognize them, until the symptoms are in front of me. And even then, there is not much anyone can do. It starts with not remembering names. Then it is dates, and that is why the calendar is so important. Then the days of the week and the months of the year. Then comes the look or stare, which appears as a blankness in Dee's eyes. At some point, I realized that I had lost my Love, at least in the thinking process. But I do not know exactly when that was. At some point, the bathroom facility becomes very important. When Dee would go to the toilet, at first, she would forget to pull her pants down. And of course I did not know when she had to go. I learned to put Dee on a schedule and to stick to it. We would make a toilet run approximately every two hours. Three hours maybe, if she had not been drinking anything. Over the time, Dee wore panties, then panties with small pads. Then panties with large pads. Next was wearing Depends, and next I added small pads to the Depends, and then big pads. For a while, Dee could make it through the night without needing any panty changing until morning. That also had to be changed, to about a 2am change. Sometimes, it is hard to remember exactly when she needs to go, but I try to make it easier, by keeping to the hour. That way I can remember a little more easily when and what I need to do.

For some time, she tried to prepare our food in between our eating out in restaurants. But as time has moved along, I needed to start ordering for her at restaurants. Eating out started to become embarrassing, Dee would make noise tapping on her plate. Then she would start talking, and then dropping food on the floor. I have seen people with babies, and young children eat at restaurants, and they would allow their children to drop food all over the floor. I do not think it is appropriate for children to be allowed to play with their food. I know that was never a possibility when I was a child and Dee had told me in the past, that when she was a child, that was her teaching too. My father would always say, "There are many hungry children around the world, who are very hungry, and they would love to have the food you wasted, or did not eat". I learned to always clean my plate, and tried not to put too much on it. I did not want Dee creating a mess with dropping her food on the floor. It has gotten now, I will only take Dee to this one coffee shop, Emily's place,where Emily is the waitress, and the clientele know Dee, and what Dee's problems are. But we make out okay. I put a bib on Dee, and have her in her transport chair, roll her as close to the table as possible. With the addition of a couple napkins, we can eliminate any food accidents. And if we should drop a few droplets, I do my best to clean them up before we leave. I do not want anyone to have to clean up a mess I felt I may have been responsible for. I am responsible for Dee.

I am sad, and feel so sad for Dee, to have to live the way she has to at this point in her life. I am sure, and I feel I know her well enough, that she would always want to be active. Dee used to read quite a lot. Especially on weekends, when she had more time. And Dee would never want anyone to have to care for her daily needs. Dee was always very private concerning her bathroom habits and needs. She would have been very angry at me, with my way of cleaning her. Each day, I have to wash her while she is in bed. I need help most of the time, it makes the process easier. But I have to expose her body, scrub it with soap and water and then put clean clothes on her. Dee usually cooperates most of the time. It is not so difficult, but I have to be very careful. I want to be sure she is clean, and does not have any soiled clothing on. I apply ointments to keep away from any sores which can develop. I am always checking for any injuries, or potential problems. After cleansing is finished, I put Dee in her transport chair, and move her to the kitchen for our breakfast.

Alzheimer's disease has robbed Dee of so much. And me too. There are so very many things Dee is missing. Going to church regularly is one. Going out to eat is another. Going grocery shopping is another. Shopping at the malls is another. Going to the casinos is another. Talking and visiting with others is another. And I could go on and on. All of these things have been taken away from Dee over the last 16 years. I see many couples walking down the street, and I think, how lucky they are. Oh yes, I can put Dee in her transport chair, and push her around the block. And Dee sometimes looks around, and sometimes sleeps, but never talks. But that is what I miss so much, being able to walk and talk with my Dee. I miss her so much!! For so many years, I took all of these walks and talks for granted. If I could only help Dee get better. I try to take as good of care of her as I can here in our home, but there is not anything I would not give up, just to have her talk to me, or even walk. I always pray for a miracle. We know Alzheimer's disease is tough, but it has taken most of Dee's life. Yes, she is eating and breathing, but all the things she always wanted to do, and people to visit, etc., this is all gone for her. The only thing left for her to lose would be her life. And I never want that to happen. I will take as good of care of Dee as I can, until I leave this earth. I must say Dee is the Love of my life, and will be forever.

Alzheimer's disease has robbed Dee. To me, it is so sad, for Dee especially, and for me too. The holidays come and go, Christmas, New Years, Birthdays, etc. and all the other holidays too. So many precious memories of each of the past celebrations, which have now gone by. All of the memories of them with Dee are happy ones. All of them made special moments, along with the special memories. So many of them, since 1967. When I look around at all the decorations, at all the things in our house and home, all the things outside and all the things stored in the garage, they all belong to Dee. Each and everyone are items and things Dee and I have collected, and accumulated. They are memories we gathered together over all these years. All our furniture, we have collected, or built. The collectables, the pictures, the cards, everything, have Dee written all over them. All this memorabilia is Dee. Everything I look at is Dee. It is amazing how much I am attached to Dee. She is my reason for living, and being here to think of her this way. It is too bad, she has to live in this bed in our dining room. To me, Dee is everything. She is the oxygen in my body. She is my heart and blood, and circulates throughout my body. But I still have her to see, and touch, and love. And I will do that, as long as I have oxygen inside me. I feel privileged to be able to love her, and care for her each moment of each day. Dee is the love of my life. This Alzheimer's has robbed Dee of her life. Dee should not have to live like this. Dee should be able to get out, see the world, travel, etc., and do all the things most Seniors do. I am 8 years older now than Dee was when she was diagnosed with this horrible disease. I try to live a somewhat normal life. I just wish Dee could be living a life like this also, instead of being locked up inside her head, by her deteriorated brain. Alzheimer's, what a thief. I feel so lost! I only wish I could help Dee get better. I wish I could put into words, the love, and expressions she gives to me, each and every day. She tries to show her love the best way she is capable of doing. If she could only lean over and give me a kiss, I would be ecstatic.

A Little More About Dee's Spiritual Life

I mentioned Dee used to read quite a lot, especially on the weekends, when she had more time. She has many spiritual books, rosary beads and prayer cards all around our home. Dee created her own little altar for some of the spiritual figures, and cards, and anything connected to her religion. Many times, I would see Dee stop, pick up a prayer card, and read it on her way to the kitchen before she would go on to do whatever she was going to do. Dee has always taken her Spiritual life very seriously. I know she loved the Nun's at Holy Rosary Church in Scranton. But, because of the stepmother, Dee would never confide in any of them. Dee did mention the name of one nun she liked best, but I cannot remember the name.

When she lived with the grandmother, Dee went into the church about every day; she went to the church by herself. Dee said she just liked to sit inside the church. I never did get to see any of the statues inside the Holy Rosary Church, but Dee talked about them quite a lot. I felt Dee had a close relationship with some of them. Dee and I have been inside some Catholic Churches which have many statues, and I imagine Holy Rosary Church in Scranton, Pennsylvania, had similar ones. One time Dee and I went to Mass at a Catholic church in Greenville, Ohio. I remember it being very white, with a lot of gold around the Altar. It was more conservative looking than the churches here in California. Dee said she did not like that type of church, she said she felt it did not feel friendly to her. But Dee did say that the statues reminded her of Holy Rosary Church. I truly think that if Dee could have stayed in Scranton, with her grandmother Palaskas, Dee would have become a Nun. Because she liked the Catholic Religion, the teachings of the Church, and the way the Nuns lived, so dedicated, and Dee would have loved that Spiritual life. But the decisions from her family changed all of that for Dee.

After Dee moved to New Jersey, the entire family of Aunt Pat's went to a Catholic church there on Sundays. Dee told me the name of the church, but I cannot remember it. But I do not think Dee was as close to her religion after she left Scranton, I do not think Dee attended any church very often, other than Sundays, until after she met me and we were married. I know Dee went to church, but she never told me anything about visiting any church during the week, to Pray. Maybe she just did not have any time, she never said. I say this, because shortly after we were married, and living in Alameda, California, there was a Catholic church just up the street from our apartment. We did attend some services there, during our time in the Navy in Alameda. After we moved to Indiana, we were so busy, we did not take time to attend any church. We were invited to some. And we did go to a service at the Catholic Church in Union City, Indiana a couple times, but not regularly. After Dee and I were married, and on our trips to southern California, Dee never mentioned anything about attending any church in that area. I know attending a church is a physical thing. But it is what a person feels all the time that makes the difference within them. And I know Dee has always been a very Spiritual person inside. As I have mentioned before, Dee could have easily become a Nun. And Dee would have been a great Nun. Dee is a very Spiritual person.

We have always gone to Catholic Churches in this area, and also when we are traveling, we attend other Catholic churches. But Dee and I are not conservative Catholics. We have had many invitations to other churches, which friends attend. We would participate with their services, and we always listened for the Word, and the messages. All religions have messages, we just have to listen for them. I truly wish Dee was well enough at this time in her life, to still be able to attend church services. But we are going to try this summer.

Pajamas

Sometimes, when I am getting my clothes out or looking in the closet, I see her clothes and mine. Over the years, I had given Dee my pajamas to wear, because they fit her better, were warmer, and easier to get on and off. Now, that sight makes me so sad. I really don't want to wear those pajamas again, but the sadness is, she may never be able to wear them again. On Wednesdays, my helper and I give Dee a shower. We now have the shower chair, thanks to my helper's suggestion. When we are finished, I can see the expression on Dee's face, and I know she appreciates, and feels better, and cleaner. Just because she cannot talk, she does communicate with me the best way she can. Dee just is the Love of my life.

Experiences

Some of the things Dee and I loved to do, I cannot remember the exact year, as there were so many of them. But Dee and I have done so many many things together. I guess this is why I love Dee so much. When I think about Dee, her life today, and her past, I wonder if I am the only person, besides her grandmothers, who truly loved Dee. It is sad not to have any happy memories of a person's childhood and as I look back at what she has told me, I just do not know how such a lovely person, being Dee, could have been mistreated. Dee is such a loving, wonderful person. I love Dee. There is nothing I would not give, to make her well.

Summary

I would like to put into words, the expressions Dee gives to me each moment of each day. It is her way of showing her Love for Life, and for me. Even with all Dee's disabilities, she is still the reason for my living. When I sit beside her on her bed, she will keep rubbing her head against my shoulder. Then I slide down, and Dee will rub my face with her head. Sometimes she blinks with both eyes, and I start blinking back to her with both my eyes. I like to wink at her too. I feel this is her way of responding, that she is here, and appreciates all I can do for her. And maybe it is her way of expressing her love for me, and for the both of us. It is amazing how much I am attached to her. Dee is everything I look at, here in our house. Dee is such a big part of my everyday life, and my desire to take the best care of her, that I am able too. Dee is Love! Somewhere I read these words, and I know I had said these before, but they are important, "I Love you more today than yesterday, and less today than tomorrow". That is so true for Dee, and myself. Dee always brings a smile to my eyes, my heart, and my feelings. Dee is Love. Dee is my Love.

Dee always liked mechanical stuffed animals. They were the kind that sang a song, plus danced and moved around. Over the years, Dee had 5 of them. But because of use, they were broken, ruined, and thrown away. I remembered this again a couple months ago. Then I purchased 3 new mechanical animals, which dance and sing. I have put them on Dee's lap recently, and turned them on. I had hoped this would help in some way, but sadly, she has no response to them. Too sad.

It is sad, but happy too, to think of all the things Dee and I used to do. All the memories and experiences. For sure, we still have each other, our home, and our memories in it. Dee may have lost her ability to talk and walk, but her Love is still here.

We will always have our memories. Dee dedicated her life to making me happy which she did and all others that she may have come in contact with. Dee made me happy. Dee will always be the Love of My Life.

And to end this book is hard to do. I do hope my readers are able to see what a wonderful person Dee is, and was. Sure, there are many other things, which we both experienced over these 54 years now. But I thought this would be the best way I could honor this beautiful person, and try my best to show you readers, the remarkable person Dee is. Dee has taught me so much, and I owe her so much too. Thank you very much for your interest. Dee is the Love of My Life! Thank You!

Ray Burk, (Stoney)

Editors

I truly want to acknowledge my editors for this book. I could never have accomplished it without their help. Eliza McKenna, Jennifer Holmes, and Ian Holmes. Thank you so much to these individuals.

Also, a big "Thank You" to Sr Barbara for suggesting I write this book.

A little about me, the author/writer.

I was born and raised on a farm in eastern central Indiana, in 1943. I finished high school in 1961. I received my draft papers in December 1963. I took my physical for the Army in January 1964. Before the Army called me, I enlisted in the Navy. In March 1964, I wanted to see the world via the Navy. I signed for a 4 year active and 2 year reserve duty time. In February of 1967, I met my Dee, and we have spent the rest of our time together up to this day. I have tried to explain most of it in this book. I have never written any book, but I wanted to try. I wanted to tell Dee's story the best I could, to honor her. Dee is the Love of My Life. Thank you.

My love and I, when we were dating

My red haired, 103 lb doll

Dee is, and always has been, a beautiful lady

Dee and I, our first apartment

My happy, lovely lady

Resting and sleeping with her kitty TC

Out in our garden with her kitty BW

Wonder what Dee is thinking, with Duchess

My Dee in her decorated kitchen

Relaxing in our new home

Dee in grandmother's 160 year old rocker

Dee in our livingroom

Dee happy at work

Dee at work surrounded by her Tweetie friends

Dee smiling on Thanksgiving, excited for dinner

Dee's kitchen, beautiful lady

Dee with her favorite kitty pin

Dee ready to go out and eat

Our dance at a friends wedding

Dee showing off her ASEB made decorations

Dee's childhood home in Scranton, PA

Dee's childhood Holy Rosary Church in Scranton, PA

Our photo in 2000

Our photo in 1975

ABOOKS

ALIVE Book Publishing and ALIVE Publishing Group
are imprints of Advanced Publishing LLC,
3200 A Danville Blvd., Suite 204, Alamo, California 94507

Telephone: 925.837.7303
alivebookpublishing.com